Learner-Oriented Teaching and Assessment in Youth

This book provides sport educators with a comprehensive, learner-centred instructional toolkit to empower children and young people in collaborative, independent learning of sport and games (SGs).

The book is unique in bringing together the various pedagogical dimensions inherent to the teaching-learning process of SGs: the instructional system (teaching strategies), the social system (interactional climate), the task system (learning tasks and activities), and the assessment (for learning) system. It also shows how to effectively involve learners as active agents in promoting more democratic learning environments and equitable interactions between sportspersons. Written by a team of experts with extensive experience of using student-centred approaches as teachers, youth coaches, teacher educators, researchers, and theorists, the book introduces key concepts and evidence-based examples of best practice, with practical instructional strategies, learning tasks, and activities included in every chapter. As the chapters of the book unfold, they teach the reader how to create game-based tasks that are suited to different learner skill levels, how to align tasks, learning goals and learner needs, and feel empowered to engage young people in creativity development activities.

Covering key themes in contemporary sport pedagogy from the constraints-led approach and appropriateness to learner-designed games and the use of technology, this is essential reading for all trainee and in-service physical education teachers and sports coaches working with children or young people.

Cláudio Farias is Senior Lecturer in the Faculty of Sport at the University of Porto (FADEUP), Portugal and a research member in the Centre of Research, Education, Innovation, and Intervention in Sport (CIFI2D). He lectures on the Doctoral Program, on the Master (hons) of PE and sports training, and on the Bachelor (hons) program in Sport Sciences. He has conducted research in sport pedagogy and sport coaching (physical education, teacher education, and coach education) with a principal focus on student-centred, model-based practice.

Isabel Mesquita is Full Professor in the Faculty of Sport at the University of Porto (FADEUP), Portugal. She is Co-ordinator for research in the area of Sport, Education, and Culture in the Centre of Research, Education, Innovation, and Intervention in Sport (CIFI2D) and in the doctoral program in Sport Sciences at FADEUP. She is also Director of the Masters in sport training and has conducted extensive research in sport pedagogy and sport coaching.

Routledge Focus on Sport Pedagogy
Series editor
Ash Casey, Loughborough University, UK

The field of sport pedagogy (physical education and coaching) is united by the desire to improve the experiences of young people and adult participants. The *Routledge Focus on Sport Pedagogy* series presents small books on big topics in an effort to eradicate the boundaries that currently exist between young people, adult learners, coaches, teachers and academics, in schools, clubs and universities. Theoretically grounded but with a strong emphasis on practice, the series aims to open up important and useful new perspectives on teaching, coaching and learning in sport and physical education.

The Game-Centred Approach to Sport Literacy
Sixto González-Víllora, Javier Fernandez-Rio, Eva Guijarro and Manuel Jacob Sierra-Díaz

Meaningful Physical Education
An Approach for Teaching and Learning
Edited by Tim Fletcher, Déirdre Ní Chróinín, Douglas Gleddie and Stephanie Beni

Pedagogies of Social Justice in Physical Education and Youth Sport
Shrehan Lynch, Jennifer L. Walton-Fisette and Carla Luguetti

Learner-Oriented Teaching and Assessment in Youth Sport
Edited by Cláudio Farias and Isabel Mesquita

For more information about this series, please visit: https://www.routledge.com/Routledge-Focus-on-Sport-Pedagogy/book-series/RFSPED

Learner-Oriented Teaching and Assessment in Youth Sport

Edited by
Cláudio Farias and Isabel Mesquita

Routledge
Taylor & Francis Group

LONDON AND NEW YORK

First published 2022
by Routledge
4 Park Square, Milton Park, Abingdon, Oxon OX14 4RN

and by Routledge
605 Third Avenue, New York, NY 10158

Routledge is an imprint of the Taylor & Francis Group, an informa business

British Library Cataloguing-in-Publication Data
A catalogue record for this book is available from the British Library

Library of Congress Cataloging-in-Publication Data
Names: Farias, Cláudio (Sport Scientist), editor. | Mesquita,
Isabel, editor.
Title: Learner-oriented teaching and assessment in youth
sport / edited by Cláudio Farias and Isabel Mesquita.
Identifiers: LCCN 2022008505 | ISBN 9780367690076 (Hardback) |
ISBN 9780367690090 (Paperback) | ISBN 9781003140016 (eBook)
Subjects: LCSH: Sports—Study and teaching. | Teamwork
(Sports)—Study and teaching | Group games—Study and teaching. |
Team sports—Study and teaching. | Coaches (Athletics)—Training
of. | Physical education teachers—Training of.
Classification: LCC GV361 .L39 2022 | DDC 796.07/1—dc23/
eng/20220406
LC record available at https://lccn.loc.gov/2022008505

ISBN: 978-0-367-69007-6 (hbk)
ISBN: 978-0-367-69009-0 (pbk)
ISBN: 978-1-003-14001-6 (ebk)

DOI: 10.4324/9781003140016

Contents

Figures

Tables

Boxes

Contributors

José Afonso is Senior Lecturer in the Faculty of Sport at the University of Porto (FADEUP), Portugal, and a research member in the Centre of Research, Education, Innovation, and Intervention in Sport (CIFI2D). He is a former volleyball coach (five National Titles, two Coach of Year Awards, Head Coach of U18 Female National Teams), and he is currently researching in Exercise Physiology and Training Methodology.

Cristiana Bessa is a Lecturer in the Faculty of Sport of the University of Porto (FADEUP) and a research member in the Centre of Research, Education, Innovation, and Intervention in Sport (CIFI2D). She lectures in Didactics, Sport Pedagogy, and Instructional methods. Within the Sports Sciences area, her main research interests are Instructional Models in Physical Education, Sport Pedagogy, and Physical Education Teacher Education.

Filipe Manuel Clemente is an assistant professor at Escola Superior de Desporto e Lazer – Instituto Politécnico de Viana do Castelo (Portugal) and research member of Instituto de Telecomunicações (Portugal). The research lines of Filipe Manuel Clemente are (i) testing and monitoring; (ii) training methodology; and (iii) performance analysis. Besides scientific activity, he also collaborates as a consultant for testing and monitoring with sports clubs and I&D companies in the area of data analytics applied in sports.

Patrícia Coutinho is Lecturer in the Faculty of Sport of the University of Porto (FADEUP), Portugal, and a research member in the Centre of Research, Education, Innovation, and Intervention in Sport (CIFI2D). She lectures in sport methodology and instructional methods. Her main research interests are long-term athlete development, sport expertise, skill acquisition, coach education, and didactics.

Pedro Tiago Esteves is Adjunct Professor at the Polytechnic Institute of Guarda, Portugal. His research focuses on the informational constraints that support goal-directed behaviours in sports. He is also intensively involved in knowledge transfer with key stakeholders such as national teams and governing bodies.

Peter A. Hastie is Full Professor and a Wayne T. Smith Distinguished Professor in the School of Kinesiology at Auburn University, USA. In 2013, Dr Hastie was inducted with Fellow status into the National Academy of Kinesiology and is a leading researcher in model-based, learner-centred pedagogies.

Ana Ramos is Lecturer in the Faculty of Sport of the University of Porto (FADEUP), Portugal, and a research member in the Centre of Research, Education, Innovation, and Intervention in Sport (CI-FI2D). Within the area of sports sciences, her research interests are related to the topics of sports training, sports pedagogy, didactics, action-research, long-term athlete development, and performance analysis.

Bruno Travassos, Universidade da Beira Interior and CIDESD – Research Center in Sports Sciences, Health Sciences and Human Development, Portugal. He is Director of the MSc in UBI and Co-ordinator of the CreativeLab Group of the CIDESD. His research activity is focused on players' decision-making, creation of representative practice tasks, and methodology of training.

Tristan L. Wallhead is Full Professor in the Division of Kinesiology and Health at the University of Wyoming, USA. Dr Wallhead conducts research on the effects of pedagogical models, such as Sport Education, on student learning and physical literacy. He serves on the board of Directors for AIESEP.

Part I

Introduction to a Learner-Oriented Approach

1 Pedagogical Principles of a Learner-Oriented Approach

Cláudio Farias and Isabel Mesquita

What is the purpose of this book?

This book aims to help sport educators[1] find teaching and coaching solutions to the following educational quest: *How can I, as a sport educator, promote the utmost motor, social, cognitive, and personal development in learners[2] through their experience of active participation in sport and games?*[3]

This leading aspiration involves not only the intention to guide learners towards an ability to play the game skilfully and towards an in-depth understanding of the internal logic of games (Storey & Butler, 2013). Beyond that, it concurrently aims at learners' active participation in the teaching-learning processes that influence their individual sport development and that of their peers (in what can be realistically expected to be the learner's best ability to master and participate in these processes) (Hastie & Mesquita, 2016). It is, therefore, a positive approach to learning since it advocates the unlimited potential of every child and their ability to transcend themselves (Whitehead, 2007) as a result of careful (and sustained) pedagogical support that trusts in young learners and in their innate and unique developmental potential.

Simply put, learners must achieve the highest level of skilful participation in sport and games through committed and active participation in the decision-making and instructional and social processes that determine their sport development.

This book, therefore, intends to provide sport educators with a comprehensive learner-oriented pedagogical toolkit designed to empower learners' collaborative, independent, democratic, and augmented learning of sport and games individually or as part of persistent learning teams. A specific set of scaffolding strategies and assessment activities are offered that show how sport educators can progressively

DOI: 10.4324/9781003140016-2

and sustainably maximize the creative, meaningful,[4] skilful, socially thoughtful, and responsible participation of sport learners in their experience of learning sport and games.

What are the main goals of this learner-oriented approach, its context of implementation, and who is it for?

The hands-on nature of the learner-oriented framework

Although the proposal we present here draws on sound evidence-based and conceptual knowledge, this proposal is *eminently practical*. It specifically provides sport educators with concrete pedagogical strategies based on goal-setting and instructional and social interventions to be applied in the real context of practice. Namely, in physical education, school sport, and in formal community-based or recreational youth sport institutions.

The learner-oriented proposal provides an evidence-based body of knowledge built through research in real practice contexts. This knowledge basis has been systematized and is now being returned to sport educators to assist in their daily teaching and coaching practice.

The wide-ranging context of application of the learner-oriented approach

We chose to focus this book on the context of sport and games and in the PE and youth sport setting. Therefore, this book includes examples of practical episodes and instructional situations, contexts, and learning tasks that seek to cover not only typical situations predominantly referenced to invasion games or net and wall games but also in striking and fielding games.

Nevertheless, given the transversal scope of this instructional proposal, we must emphasize that sport educators can easily apply most of the components of this book (Chapters 3–6, 9, or 10–12) in different sport fields (e.g., dance, gymnastics, athletics, Outdoor Adventure Activities) and contexts of sport practice (school, sport training), and with different age groups (e.g., adult sport).

The wide-ranging beneficiaries of a learner-oriented approach

The most obvious beneficiaries of this approach are children. The conditions are in place so that their participation in sport and games becomes a remarkable experience in their lives (Farias, Wallhead, &

Mesquita, 2020). Namely, the learner-oriented approach can have a memorable impact on young people's development in all educational domains (motor, social, and personal) and in their willingness to participate in sport activities (Silva, Farias, & Mesquita, 2021).

Sport educators will also be the most direct beneficiaries of this learner-oriented experience. This proposal can also be an appropriate tool for teacher educators and for their training of future PE teachers and for the professional development of in-service teachers. The marked focus on very practical teaching strategies can encourage both experienced teachers and novice teachers to involve students more actively in the teaching-learning process.

This proposal could be also very useful for the coach education context, i.e., for students aspiring to be coaches in academic coach-oriented training and for their teachers in the higher education courses.

Finally, researchers may have a good opportunity to put the learner-oriented pedagogical strategies provided here in action to develop new knowledge about teaching and coaching processes and their effect on the learning of sport and games.

The pedagogical features of a learner-oriented approach

The term 'learner-oriented' was purposely chosen for two main reasons:

i The unique sporting, cultural, and social experience and skills of each learner are placed at the heart of the planning of children's experience of learning sport and games.
ii Since the teaching-learning process is, as far as reasonably possible, 'oriented' (driven) by the learners themselves, the sport educator becomes a facilitator of learning through scaffolding strategies.

In the same way, scaffolding can be seen as a practical metaphor with a twofold purpose. On the one hand, the book offers a wide range of instructional strategies through which the sport educator can progressively support the active participation of learners in building their learning experience. This includes explicit tools for mediating the quality of social interactions taking place between learners (Chapter 5). The nurturing climate generated through such positive social interactions will impact positively on the quality of instruction to increase the potential for children to learn more efficiently from the sport educator and from each other.

On the other hand, each chapter progressively supports the professional development of sport educators in their promotion of increasingly more democratic sport learning contexts. Chapter by chapter, sports educators are 'scaffolded' to actively engage learners in increasingly complex learning processes (as players, peer-coaches, or as game designers). Sport educators are shown how to progress in their ability to gradually transfer decision-making power and responsibility to learners. This is a high point for teachers and coaches who wish to innovate their practices because it allows them to maintain a high sense of control and ownership of the process of sharing and transferring 'power' to learners.

That is, the scaffolding strategies help sport educators to progress from the ability to mediate collaborative learning among learners (Chapter 4) to the ability to promote successful peer-learning interactions or the active engagement of learners in building positive social behaviours (Chapters 5 or 11). Sport educators can also progress from the ability to design tasks for promoting game-play development through discovery-based activities (Chapter 7) and creative thinking (Chapter 8) to the ability to facilitate the construction of inventive learner-led games (Chapter 9).

What is the type of engagement and instructional dynamics in a learner-oriented approach?

This learner-oriented approach acknowledges the importance of considering the typical demands present in any adult-led site of youth development through and in sport. Even when learners are expected to have an active voice in the teaching-learning process (i.e., leadership of instructional processes such as task presentation or peer-assessment), the pedagogical goal-setting and degree of relevance of the experiences lived by learners will always need to be planned, facilitated, and monitored by the adult – the sport educator. In short, whatever the nature of the scaffolding put in place by the sport educator (e.g., through more or less explicit instruction) and the degree to which learners are more or less actively involved in this process, they will always need to have some adult guidance.

Therefore, the main pedagogical avenues for the full achievement of the learner-oriented educational experience will involve:

- The sport educator acting as a facilitator of learning. The ultimate aim of the sport educator is to facilitate the highest development of the learner (multidimensional: motor, cognitive, social, and affective outcomes) with their highest active involvement in the construction of the learning experience.

- The extensive promotion of peer-assisted, peer-teaching, and peer-assessment activities.
- The extensive promotion of collaborative learning experiences (empowering learners as collective problem-solvers).
- The extensive promotion of discovery-learning activities aimed at the development of critical thinking and high cognitive engagement.
- The extensive participation in activities that develop sound social awareness (inclusion, acceptance of difference, empathy), inclusive attitudes, and equity in learners' participation in sport-based activities.
- The progressive transfer of decision-making power to learners and their increasing ownership of the learning experience (learning how to learn and teach each other sport and games).

Box 1.1 Key concept: peer-coaching

In this proposal, 'peer-coaching' is deemed to be a more all-embracing term than 'peer-teaching'. Peer-coaching can be used both in PE and in youth sport contexts. Further, peer-coaching can involve more than teaching content to peers. It may include active peer counselling and mediation of social relationships between team members. In this case, the term 'peer-leader' is also representative.

Box 1.2 Key point: educational benefits of peer-teaching and collaborative sport-based activities

The present learner-oriented approach draws heavily on peer-coaching and collaborative learning activities. There are numerous known educational benefits of learner involvement in these pedagogies.
  From a peer-leader perspective:

Learners develop a more refined understanding of sport content
    because they need to interpret and verbalize sport content

(e.g., the content of task cards) so that such information can be grasped, and the task can be successfully performed by their peers.

Learners become more sensitive toward, and aware of, the diverse strengths, weaknesses, and learning needs of peers with different learning needs.

The prolonged participation in peer-coaching activities has transformative potential in these learners, who consciously transfer to the sports club some positive leadership and sport culture behaviours that are developed during physical education lessons.

To learners, in general:

Learners seem to benefit from participation in communication styles that are cognitively, culturally, and socially aligned with their level of understanding.

The exchange of knowledge and understanding between learners always entails an increase in social ties between them.

Collaborative and peer-coaching interactions implicitly demonstrate signs of concern, affection, and recognition of group identity of the involved children.

Where is this learner-oriented approach inspired from and what does it offer?

This learner-oriented approach fairly draws on some of the pedagogical features of well-established pedagogical models (e.g., Sport Education, Siedentop, Hastie, & Van der Mars, 2019; Tactical Games model, Mitchell, Oslin, & Griffin, 2020; or Cooperative Learning, Dyson & Casey, 2016). These features include peer-teaching, sport role-playing, accountability systems, collaborative problem-solving in learning teams, and cooperative activities for positive interdependence and social skills development.

Although this proposal revisits seminal conceptions of student-centred pedagogies (Dyson, Griffin, & Hastie, 2004), it expands the scope of the educational outcomes developed by learners through their expanded engagement in decision-making activities usually led or mediated exclusively by the teacher or coach. In this sense, this learner-oriented proposal reflects a reconciled integration of several pedagogical domains: instructional (Farias, Hastie & Mesquita, 2018; Rink, 2014; Xun & Land, 2004), ecological (Davids, Button, & Bennett, 2008; Lund, 1992), cognitive and creative complexity (Storey & Butler, 2013), and meaningful theory (Beni, Fletcher, & Ní Chróinín, 2017).

Box 1.3 Key concept: Cooperative and collaborative learning

Cooperative learning (Dyson & Casey, 2016) is a pedagogical model historically and firmly confirmed in the field of PE and sport pedagogy. In a very short way, Cooperative learning contains a set of very rich and systematized teaching and learning structures and dynamics and generally focuses on working in an interdependent fashion, where each member of the group is often responsible for a 'piece' of the final product. Cooperative learning (Dyson & Casey, 2016, p. 4) also promotes considerable Face-to-Face Interaction, clearly perceived Individual Accountability and personal responsibility to achieve the group's goals, frequent use of the relevant Interpersonal and Small Group Skills, and frequent and regular Group Processing of current functioning to improve the group's future effectiveness.

Cooperative learning is an important inspiration for the present learner-oriented approach. For example, its principles are expressed in practical tasks present throughout for attending to learners' intra-individual and inter-individual variability (see Chapters 6 or 8), positive interdependence (see Chapter 5), and more democratic participation of all learners in the sporting experience (see Chapters 9 or 11).

Nonetheless, overall, we pursue a more open form of cooperative activities that will be more commensurate with the notion of collaborative learning. Collaborative problem-solving and learning tends to feature more fluid, shifting roles, with group members crossing boundaries between different areas of work, or co-deciding the best ways to collaborate on their joint project (Laal & Laal, 2012).

This learner-oriented approach proposes that sport educators act as facilitators of learning, and that they gradually shift responsibility to learners. This book makes a significant contribution to the field in that it provides an exhaustive framework of scaffolding strategies through which the sport educator can successfully put into practice the role of facilitator, at different levels of active involvement of learners and of the responsibility that is transferred to them (see for example Chapters 3–5).

We highlight an additional set of potential attributes of this book that sport learners, in-service teachers and coaches, future teachers and coaches, and teacher and coach educators might appreciate:

- This learner-oriented approach brings together various pedagogical dimensions critical to the teaching-learning process related to sport and games; the instructional system (teaching strategies), the social system (interactional climate), the task system (learning tasks and activities), and the assessment (for learning) system (Rink, 2020).
- It can be a valuable practical tool to support and maximize the teaching of PE through model-based PE (Sport Education, Cooperative Learning; Game-based approaches; Tannehill, Van der Mars, & MacPhail, 2013).
- It offers a more flexible and progressive interplay between the teaching and coaching instruction and the level of learners' engagement in the learning activities. It goes beyond any specific 'fixed' and 'non-negotiable' set of teacher or learner behaviour benchmarks. The learner is asked to perform, and the respective tools are used to help them, according to their stage of development in the learner-oriented experience. For example, learners teach more complex tasks to peers if they are prepared to do so and not because it is mandatory that they participate in peer-teaching tasks.
- It progressively locates the different roles and level of responsibility assumed by sport educators and sport learners in decision-making related to different instructional dimensions (i.e., content selection, problem and solution selection or identification, task design and presentation, task assessment and feedback).
- It applies knowledge from other sports science disciplines that interface with sport pedagogy to extend sport educators' comprehension and ability to build (or facilitate the learner's building of) developmentally appropriate learning tasks and promote learners' development of creativity skills.

How do we think learners' sport development happens?

The teaching methods applied in any pedagogical approach to teaching sport and games are always underpinned by specific assumptions on how children and young people learn. The present learner-oriented approach values the *Intrapersonal, Social interactional, and Interdependent* dimensions of learning.

Intrapersonal dimension of learning

The ability of human beings to express themselves through bodily movements is untransmissible because no one has the capacity to learn and move in 'someone's place'. In addition, two learners may be looking at the same situation, or may be performing an identical task, but they may be interpreting and expressing that understanding in completely different ways. This means that the learning process has a strong intrapersonal dimension.

The following assumptions about the intrapersonal dimension of learning are highlighted:

- Learning is a process in which the learner constructs unique knowledge through the projection of their life history of experiences, and the interaction of their previous experience and knowledge with the new experience and to-be-learned task.
- Learning involves an active interpretation of the events by the individual, which is shaped by experience and through exploration, discovery, activation, and reorganization of existing knowledge to make a unique understanding of the new situation.
- Learning is a process of adapting to and fitting into a constantly changing world where understanding arises from the learner's engagement in the world through perception, motor action, and bodily senses.
- Meaningful sport experiences are intrinsically personal. They rely on the interplay between the learner's skills and their own learning goals and aspirations, which are closely linked to each learner's 'life history'.

Box 1.4 Key point: practical implications of the intrapersonal dimension of learning

- Sport educators should consider the unique features, motivations, experiences, and knowledge-background of sport learners to successfully design meaningful sporting experiences.

- Be aware that learning experience becomes representative to students when the sport educator creates contexts that value the unique and innate capabilities of different learners (e.g., through accountability strategies or tailor-made learning tasks and assessment) or generates positive social interactions among students that will enable their access to a fuller participation in the learning experience.

The social interactional dimension of learning

Learning also holds a strong social interactional dimension:

- Learning is an intra-individual process but it is also a social process in which the development of various knowledgeable learners is inseparably involved with each other.
- As learners develop their ability to communicate and share common interpretations with their peers about sport and games, they also become progressively more likely to participate in sport, games, and physical activity.
- Learning involves learners' progression in the trajectories of full participation in the social and instructional life of the community of learners (e.g., class, team, learning team) to which they belong.
- As the collective constructions of belonging to a community of learners evolve, and each of its members is accepted by their peers for the unique contribution they make to the group, it increases the disposition of all members to share knowledge and provide democratic access to the knowledge resources contained in that learning community.
- There is an interrelated development between learners' mutual trust, caring, and sensitivity towards individual differences, their disposition to share knowledge and pursue more equitable and democratic learning goals as a group, and the level of participation in the group activities of each learner.

Box 1.5 Key point: practical implications of the social interactional dimension of learning

- Sport educators are encouraged to gradually shift responsibility to learners for the active participation in instructional (e.g., learner-led selection of game-play tasks) and

decision-making dynamics (e.g., deciding on the strategies and tasks to be practiced by the learning teams).
- Sport educators are encouraged to promote extensive participant of learners in persistent learning teams.
- This offers children the opportunity to plan, practice, and benefit from the social development opportunities implicit in their engagement in team membership learning activities.
- The success of any instructional interaction taking place between learners is always influenced by the 'quality' of the social interactions that mediate their knowledge interchanges.

The interdependent dimension of learning

Human development and learning are also conceived as a process that is heavily (and interdependently) influenced by several contextual (environment and task conditions), socio-cultural (in the construction of meanings with others), and physical-perceptual (cognitive, emotional, and physical characteristics of the individual) dimensions (Hastie & Mesquita, 2016). To highlight a few examples:

- How learners interpret the expectations that others have in relation to their motor skills, personal characteristics, or 'status' position in the group, greatly influences what will be the actual motor performance and social identity of that learner.
The type of learning climate encouraged by the sport educator (e.g., is the 'error' a reason for punishment or is overcoming it a core learning goal?) and the collective constructions of what it means to be competent in that group heavily influences learners' perceptions of how good and successful they are.
- Motor performance expresses interdependent interactions between learners. For example, good passing depends, and is influenced by the nature of social relationships between learners; healthy and socially positive interactions lead to inclusive and equitable participation of learners.
- Learning is also influenced by an interdependent relationship between performer (height, expertise, or the emotional state of the learner), environment (in meteorological conditions, performing in front of an audience), and task (e.g., goals, rules, or equipment) conditions.
- During learners' game-play, they couple their 'reading' of the context with their motor actions in a process of exploring appropriate

movement solutions within the possibilities for action provided by the situational circumstances faced at that moment.

Box 1.6 Key point: practical implications of the interdependent dimension of learning

Sport educators are encouraged to gradually shift responsibility to learners for the active participation in instructional (e.g., learner-led selection of game-play tasks) and decision-making dynamics (e.g., deciding on the strategies and tasks to be practiced by the learning teams).

Sport educators are encouraged to create a learning climate markedly aimed at establishing self-referenced and assessment learning activities and task goals that acknowledge intra- and inter-individual variability.

Accountability systems and recognition of competence at a multidimensional level (underlying motor, personal, and social achievement) should be in place.

Notes

1 In this book, the term Sport Educator includes all physical education and school sport teachers and community-based sport coaches, and all practitioners invested in the education of children and young people through and in sport and games.

2 The terms learner and sport learner are indistinctly used in this book. It is an all-encompassing term that includes any young person who is learning sport and games. They refer to physical education and school sport learners and sport practitioners in the youth sport coaching settings.

3 The concept of sport and games simultaneously comprises individual and team sports in their formal versions and all forms of small-sided modified games and game practice of more, or less, formal versions of sport (Gréhaigne, Richard, & Griffin, 2012).

4 Meaningful learning of sport and games emphasizes shared positive participation (social interactions), 'just-right' sport engagement challenges that afford opportunities for learning (increased motor competence), fun (encompass immediate enjoyment), and delight (experiencing more sustained pleasure or joy as a result of significant engagement and commitment in sporting activities; Beni, Fletcher, & Ní Chróinín, 2017).

References

Beni, S., Fletcher, T., & Ní Chróinín, D. (2017). Meaningful experiences in physical education and youth sport: A review of the literature. *Quest, 69*(3), 291–312.

Davids, K., Button, C., & Bennett, S. (2008). *Dynamics of skill acquisition: A constraints-led approach*. Champaign, IL: Human Kinetics Publishers.

Dyson, B., & Casey, A. (2016). *Cooperative learning in physical education and physical activity: A practical introduction*. London: Routledge.

Dyson, B., Griffin, L. L., & Hastie, P. (2004). Sport education, tactical games, and cooperative learning: Theoretical and pedagogical considerations. *Quest, 56*(2), 226–240.

Farias, C., Hastie, P. A., & Mesquita, I. (2018). Scaffolding student–coaches' instructional leadership toward student-centred peer interactions: A year-long action-research intervention in sport education. *European Physical Education Review, 24*(3), 269–291.

Farias, C., Wallhead, T., & Mesquita, I. (2020). "The project changed my life": Sport education's transformative potential on student physical literacy. *Research Quarterly for Exercise and Sport, 91*(2), 263–278.

Gréhaigne, J. F., Richard, J. F., & Griffin, L. L. (2012). *Teaching and learning team sports and games*. New York: Routledge.

Hastie, P. A., & Mesquita, I. (2016). Sport-based physical education *(1st edition)*. In C. Ennis (Ed.), *Routledge handbook of physical education pedagogies* (pp. 86–102). Champaign, IL: Routledge.

Laal, M., & Laal, M. (2012). Collaborative learning: What is it? *Procedia-Social and Behavioral Sciences, 31*, 491–495.

Lund, J. (1992). Assessment and accountability in secondary physical education. *Quest, 44*(3), 352–360.

Mitchell, S., Oslin, J., & Griffin, L. L. (2020). *Teaching sport concepts and skills: A tactical games approach*. Champaign, IL: Human Kinetics Publishers.

Rink, J. E. (2020). *Teaching physical education for learning* (8th edition). Boston, MA: McGraw Hill Education.

Siedentop, D., Hastie, P., & Van der Mars, H. (2019). *Complete guide to sport education* (3rd edition). Champaign, IL: Human Kinetics.

Silva, R., Farias, C., & Mesquita, I. (2021). Cooperative learning contribution to student social learning and active role in the class. *Sustainability, 13*(15), 1–18.

Storey, B., & Butler, J. (2013). Complexity thinking in PE: Game-centred approaches, games as complex adaptive systems, and ecological values. *Physical Education and Sport Pedagogy, 18*(2), 133–149.

Tannehill, D., Van der Mars, H., & MacPhail, A. (2013). *Building effective physical education programs*. Burlington, MA: Jones & Bartlett Publishers.

Whitehead, M. (2007). Physical literacy: Philosophical considerations in relation to developing a sense of self, universality and propositional knowledge. *Sport, Ethics and Philosophy, 1*(3), 281–298.

Xun, G. E., & Land, S. M. (2004). A conceptual framework for scaffolding III-structured problem-solving processes using question prompts and peer interactions. *Educational Technology Research and Development, 52*(2), 5–22.

2 Guidelines for Navigating a Learner-Oriented Approach

Cláudio Farias and Isabel Mesquita

How to navigate a learner-oriented approach?

Part I ("Introduction to a learner-oriented approach") in this book (Chapters 1 and 2) presents the central pedagogical principles and rationale of this learner-oriented approach. In Chapter 1 we provide key information on the core pedagogies and target educational outcomes of this approach. We also clarify the assumptions held on how the learning of sport and games takes place and we establish a link with the pedagogical interactions and activities offered in this proposal. Chapter 2 briefly puts together the overall structure of the learner-oriented approach.

Part II ("Scaffolding mediation of instructional and social interactions in sport and games") covers the instructional processes that sport educators can put in place to scaffold (mediate) the instructional and social interactions taking place between sport educators and learners, and between learners themselves. Overall, the instructional strategies presented in Part II provide the practical and supportive backbone for implementing the pedagogies presented in Part III. Chapter 3 explains what scaffolding is and outlines the scaffolding intentions, means, settings, and teaching/coaching strategies. We also show how responsibility can be gradually transferred to students in their increasing participation in the learning and teaching of sport and games. Chapter 4 provides a more practical application of the general operations defined in Chapter 3. Three levels of mediation of instructional interactions are presented: (a) scaffolding general instructional interactions; (b) scaffolding collaborative instructional interactions; and (c) scaffolding learner-led instructional interactions.

Chapter 5 moves on to show how sport educators can mediate the quality of social interactions occurring between learners. Sport educators receive explicit guidance on the proactive building of

DOI: 10.4324/9781003140016-3

more democratic, ethically responsible, and meaningful learning environments.

Part III ("Designing meaningful and creative learning activities in sport and games") is explicitly focused on content development and activity and task design. Chapter 6 states the main conceptual principles that are put into practice in the following chapters. A visit is made to the central foundations of the instructional process in teaching sport and games. There is an emphasis on the need to organize learning goals and learning tasks according to the individual characteristics of every learner to generate more meaningful learning experiences for all. Chapters 7–9 unfold in a progressive engagement and ownership of learners in the teaching–learning process. Chapter 7 shows how sport educators can modify and manipulate learning tasks across different game categories considering the individual and collective learning needs of sport learners. Chapter 8 addresses the dimension of creativity to expand the participation of learners in playing games and learning about games. Chapter 9 provides guidelines on how to extend the connection between the experience of designing and playing games and the learners' wider cultural world. Learners will assume the leadership of designing game-based learning activities.

Finally, Part IV ("Learner-Oriented Assessment") includes three chapters. Chapter 10 highlights the various dimensions of the teaching-assessment-learning cycle showing how sport educators can make assessment a richer educational process. Chapter 11 takes into account the intra- and inter-individual variability of learners to present assessment indicators that will raise the educational experience of sport educators and learners. Finally, Chapter 12 shows how sport educators can use technology, peer-, and self-assessment strategies in the teaching and learning of sport and games.

Part II

Scaffolding Mediation of Instructional and Social Interactions in Sport and Games

3 Scaffolding as a Pedagogical Toolkit for Learner-Oriented Instruction

Cláudio Farias and Isabel Mesquita

Box 3.1 Objectives

At the end of this chapter, you will be able to:

- Understand what scaffolding is and how can it be used to improve your teaching and coaching.
- Appropriately apply different scaffolding, in different settings, to promote different levels of learner engagement.
- Identify different levels of transfer of responsibility to learners.

Box 3.2 Key sections

- Introduction
- Scaffolding intentions and means
- Scaffolding settings and operations
- Contingency: fitting the scaffolding to the situation
- Gradual transfer of responsibility to learners.

Introduction

In a learner-oriented approach, learners are expected to develop not only physical-motor outcomes but also to accomplish social, cognitive, and personal goals. In this set-up, the sport educator will need to rethink more directive and authoritarian traditional instructional practices (Hastie & Mesquita, 2016). Instead, they should embody the role of facilitator in learners' sport development. It is critical that the sport educator masters different instructional strategies that go

DOI: 10.4324/9781003140016-5

beyond the transmission of sport content. In addition, the pedagogical action of the facilitator walks together with the concepts of "zone of proximal development" (ZPD) and "scaffolding" (Vygotsky, 1978). Understanding the pedagogical functioning of these concepts allows sport educators to successfully play their role as facilitators.

In this sense, we could say that sport educators operate in a "support zone" (ZPD) located between what a learner can already do unaided (e.g., tactical skills) and what they cannot do independently but have potential to perform if given adequate support, implicit or explicit, from sport educators or a more experienced teammate.[1]

Box 3.3 Key concept: the prime goal of scaffolding

Scaffolding intends to gradually bring sport learners to a condition in which they achieve internalized and collectively built understanding-in-action and can complete a task independently as well as their ability to apply those skills to autonomously solve new practice situations.

We can identify an instructional process as scaffolding if it involves: (i) a contingent and temporary practical intervention; (ii) a fading of the support provided, either in its frequency (quantity of feedback provided) or nature (more or less explicit information); and (iii) the consequent transfer of responsibility to learners.

Table 3.1 provides an example of progressive instruction in which the level of explicit instruction provided to learners to solve a given game problem is gradually faded. Thus, the greater the learner's active engagement in understanding the best response to a particular set of game circumstances, the more the learner is held responsible for building their learning experience. Likewise, the more complex the perceptual cues (involving not only individual responses but their coordination with the opponents and teammates) and the web of if-then relationships (e.g., "*if* all teammates are tagged, *then* I should either hold the ball or attack the basket") that learners are encouraged to understand, the greater their cognitive and physical-motor effort will have to be. The success in learners' actions will necessarily depend on their ability to grasp such relationships and trigger efficient and adequate motor responses. Table 3.1[2] shows how the means of instruction selected by sport educators can be conditioned, for example, by learners' current level of problem-solving skills.

Table 3.1 Explicitness of instruction according to learner ability level

Learner ability level	Invasion games	Net games	Striking/batting games
		Less explicit support	
3 advanced	Why did we score? How is our attacker getting free all the time?	What's happening when you serve down court? (usually scores when the ball drops in between zone 5/6)!	What's happening when you're batting to the third base? (the infielders can't cut the lead runner)
2 intermediate	Why is that? So what (to do)? Someone is getting open on the left court lane (player 15).	There is a gap between two players their (between zone 5/6). Can you spot it?	There is a gap between two infielders there (between zone second/third base). Can you spot it?
1 beginner	Pass to player 15, he's wide open!	Serve the ball dropping it between zone 5/6!	Hit the ball to the left side of the field!
		More explicit support	

Responsibility increase

Fading of explicit support

Scaffolding intentions and means

Scaffolding intentions

The central goal of a learner-oriented pedagogy is to lead learners to successful participation in sport and games in an independent self-regulated manner while concurrently promoting their fullest participation in collaborative problem-solving and instructional decision-making, at the highest possible level of complexity[3] (Xun & Land, 2004).

Among many possibilities, the *scaffolding intentions* of the sport educators may include the goal to promote affective (learner's emotional self-regulation), cognitive (learner's deep understanding of the learning experience), or metalevel (learner's ability to learn how to learn) development. Several scaffolding intentions are presented below.

Recruiting and managing contingency and frustration: getting learners interested in an activity and helping them adhere to the requirements of the task. Facilitate learner performance via a system of rewards as well as keeping them motivated via the prevention or reduction of frustration.

Box 3.4 Task: bat and ball game

Conditions: 3 players (one is the batter and two are outfielders) in a triangle-shaped field (two spot markers are fence spots, one is a home base spot).

Goals: the batter should try to score as many throw-runs as possible by landing a ball beyond the fence spots. In this case, the achievement of the main objective of the game absolutely depends on the level of acuity and commitment of the outfielders (hypothetically placed in a less "appealing" role), otherwise the game will lose flow.

Accountability strategies: outfielders score points for their demonstrated effort, perseverance, and camaraderie to one another.

Note: the regular introduction in the seasons of formal moments of recognition of different merit (the player who evolved the most, or the most honest referee are recognized as the best scorers) helps to legitimize different levels of competence and removes pressure on the less able to self-assess exclusively in reference to the best performers.

Structuring Understanding: establishing a bridge between content sets (transfer of learning) or providing explanatory and belief structures that organize and justify the learning content.

Box 3.5 Task: explanation of the teaching-learning process

Explaining to learners how exactly a to-be-introduced modified game form is shaped[1] to solve specific game problems felt during game-play of a more mature game, or interrupting game-play when a specific situation arises that can be resolved through the tactical movements just practiced/discovered in the previous task (connecting content across tasks).

Managing the Degrees of Freedom: temporarily taking over those parts of a task that the learner is not yet able to perform independently.

Box 3.6 Task: managing the level of support provided

When presenting to learners the structure of a task (e.g., how the task will be organized – space, circuit, pairs, practice time, rotation of functions), combining schematic drawings on a whiteboard with verbal instruction requires less cognitive implication for the learner than the provision of this information only through verbal instruction. This way, the educator takes care of some steps in the learner's understanding of the task by removing a certain degree of abstraction with the schematic drawings.

The educator can also narrow the focus of peer-coaching interventions to specific elements in the task ("forget the rest, simply focus on how they place their fingers in the overhand throw") or, when a task is repeated, the educator can deliberately leave information out (e.g., not mentioning how learners should rotate at each trial) to prompt learners to transfer knowledge from prior sessions to the current situation.

Maintaining Direction: keeping the learner on target and maintaining their pursuit of a particular learning goal.

Box 3.7 Task: keeping learners on track

To trigger learners' identification of significant problems and errors arising from their team's game-play practice, the sport educator can integrate these processes into the pacing and transition between tasks. In a 3v3 invasion game, (1) 10-min is allocated for uninterrupted free play, (2) followed by 2-min between transition to debate about major problems perceived by learners, (3) and new game session where peer-coaches are encouraged to interrupt the game to correct their peers (e.g., not using the target-hand during support moves) or to propose possible solutions to emerging problems (e.g., cutting rapidly to the target after a side pass). The sport educator can steer the focus of the lesson towards achieving both game-play tactical skills and learners' instructional improvement.

Scaffolding means

Driven by different scaffolding intentions, sport educators can apply a wide range of *scaffolding means*. These can be represented by discrete instructional strategies. Also, the intervention of sport educators may vary from using more guidance-based instruction (e.g., demonstration, explanation, instructions) to employing more discovery-based strategies (questioning, cueing, and using indirect teaching strategies, modifying tasks for promoting exploratory-based learning; Van de Pol, Volman, & Beishuizen, 2010).

As learners become increasingly engaged in instructional decision-making, the sport educators' intervention will have a dual concern: (1) clarifying the task for the whole group; and (2) channelling the attention of peer-coaches to the main emerging problems and to the most appropriate feedback cues.

As represented in Table 3.2 (*Instructional scaffolding strategies*), the scaffolding means may range from an (almost) total control of the decision-making process by the sport educator (more explicit intervention) to a control shared with or led largely by learners themselves (more implicit intervention, see Box 8.3 and Figure 3.1) (Smit et al., 2013).

Table 3.2 Instructional scaffolding strategies

Scaffolding instructional strategies

	Means	Features	Examples
Implicit instruction	Context exploring-based (Modifications)	The educator provides information only on general task organization. Modifications are made to the task that allow learners to explore different movement solutions and to trigger the emergence of the motor behaviours learners are intended to develop.	(Water polo) In a shooting practice, the coach can place a barrier formed by fitballs in the water at different angles and distances from the goals. Without receiving explicit instruction on it, practitioners will have to explore ways to perform impulsion movements and shoot at the goal with increased effort to overcome the "constraints" placed in the context. Having fitballs of different shapes and dimensions invites each practitioner to discover the situation that best suits their possibilities of action at that moment.
	Cues and hints (plus indirect instruction)	The educator deliberately holds information about exactly what is missing in players' responses. Learners are expected to find ways to succeed based on as little information as possible. The amount of more explicit guidance provided depends on the learner's response, as she moves away, or closer to a functional solution. Indirect teaching strategies like the use of task cards may fit here. Although learners may receive explicit written instruction on key learning cues, they still need to make sense of that information to convey it properly to their peers.	(Rugby) "It seems that the pass is not coming out in the best conditions. Note the positioning of the open-side flanker and his second row back up. What's wrong there? How can we explore that gap? Let's try it... Hmm, that move didn't work. Why is that? what can we do differently? Now note how he places his feet before moving up the ball."

(Continued)

Scaffolding instructional strategies

	Means	Features	Examples
	Questioning	The use of reflective questions prompts the learner to verbalize ideas and activate cognitive perceptual-action processes (e.g., understanding, establishing if-then relationships between the configuration of the play situation and an appropriate motor response).	(Tennis) "What do we need to do to perform a good backhand shot? When should we push the opponent down court or release the pressure? How do we need to position ourselves when facing a strong backhand player? Why?"
	Instructing	If the learner is familiar with the presented motor skill/tasks, it may not be necessary to repeat the entire task model (demonstration). The learner is "forced" to draw on and transfer prior knowledge into the new situation to complete the information (visual model) not provided by the educator.	(Archery) "Last week you learned to score and record your results during the tournament target shooting. We will repeat that task but now, simply shoot from the 30-meter spot, not the 20-meter."
Explicit instruction	Explaining	Although using verbal instruction alone, the educator provides context on "how to do it" but also the "why" and "when to do it". The learner is provided with an explanatory basis of the task goals work and content development process, which can later support their self-regulation and autonomy during task practice. Usually, full details on the task critical components are provided.	(Football) "In the last match we struggled to get open inside the box. Today we'll work on mobility, create space between the central-back and wing-back. Note how we are transferring this drill to the game, the cones delimit the space left open when we pretend to pass sideways."
	Demonstrating	The learners are provided with a complete visual demonstration (the total model) of what they must do at each moment of the task. The information is complemented with verbal instruction as the educator runs through the full explanation of the task.	(Volleyball) The coach demonstrates the setting (overhand pass), at the exact spot where players should position themselves, clarifies the specific critical components of the skill (ball contact over the forehead, fingers/hands push straight through the ball towards the intended target, etc.), shows how/where players should rotate after the pass.

Box 3.8 Task: indirect teaching strategies (task card)

Example Peer Coaching Task Card: Touch Rugby 2v1
Task Goal: pair of attackers tries to beat the single defender to score past the try line.

The following example portrays a possible indirect teaching strategy (task card) that operationalizes the scaffolding of the educator through the provision of teaching cues. The scaffolding cues may include the provision of direct peer-mediated tasks that includes task cards that explain the expected motor responses and their relationship to the conditions imposed by the game. The peer coaches are responsible for reading the coaching task cards to teammates before the teams' game practice sessions and for monitoring teammates' gameplay. Figure 3.1 provides an example of a 2v1 touch rugby task card that includes the organizational components and expected solutions to the game problem.

Organization:

Groups of three players
All players wear tags
Attackers in pairs
One defender defending try line starts in middle of grid
One ball per pair of attackers

Coaching Feedback Cues:
"Run forward quickly and take the space the defender gives you"
"Pass the ball with two hands and across your body"
"Support player be ready with target hands"
"Ball carrier look where you are passing"
"Don't pass too early wait for the defender to commit to you"
"Support player keep distance and don't get in front of ball carrier"

Scaffolding settings and operations

From a teaching or coaching perspective, regardless of whether sport educators enact more or less implicit means to scaffold the occurring instructional interactions (demonstration, explanation, indirect teaching, cues), they need to create a series of learning dynamics to mediate

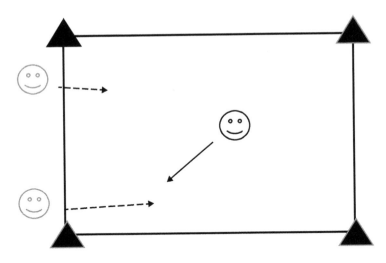

Figure 3.1 Schematic drawing of the task card.

these pedagogical interactions (King, 1992). We present below several scaffolding settings and procedures that can be used to mediate the active participation of learners in different key instructional operations related to games teaching (problem/error identification, content and task selection, task design, task presentation, feedback, and performance assessment).

Guided practice

The sport educator selects a group of peer-leaders to actively participate in a guided practice presentation. They will then lead the task implementation in their groups. The educator and the peer-coaches provide a full demonstration of the task and model each piece of information and expected movement patterns to the whole class prior to the learners establishing the tasks within their own teams. As peer-coaches actively engage in the active demonstration of the task to the whole group and experience the motor actions first-hand, they become more closely familiar with the critical components of the task. This will later guide them both in the task presentation to their peers and in their peer-feedback during the task practice.

In-task intervention

During task practice, sport educators step in and provide instruction to fix the lack of alignment between the task goals and learners' performance, or the inability of the peer-coaches to identify errors and provide feedback to their teammates. This intervention aims at restating the sport content in new ways and to reorganize and partition it in simpler parts through examples and demonstrations.

Guided task structure

The educator provides a demonstration of the task structure to the peer-coaches in a neutral court prior to the learners' implementation of those tasks within their own teams and practice spots.

Pre-lesson/post-session briefings

The briefing events take place immediately before the beginning of the sessions to support the subsequent intervention of the learners who will be responsible for leading the task practice of their teams. Depending on the level of responsibility the educator intends to transfer to learners at that moment, these interactions may serve different purposes:

- Check learners' understanding of task content and structure.
- Recall key teaching cues.
- Link content and tasks progression (e.g., clarify the relationship between the presented tasks and the emerging problems in the main game form).
- Prompt the development of argumentation and reflexive skills (e.g., "Why select task A or B? How does that help your team? What tactical skills are refined in that task?").
- Involve learners in video analysis of their teams' game-play (e.g., observing and identifying the main emerging problems).
- Cooperate with the sport educator to design and test appropriate learning tasks before presenting them to teammates.
- Model instructional interventions (e.g., practicing question-asking instruction, setting the focus, and timing of instruction intervention).

Guided observation

Guided observation intends to fade (or even replace) the in-task interventions carried out by sport educators during learners' game-play practice. Guided observation aims at transferring the in-task interventions to learners themselves (e.g., to peer-coaches). Instead of interfering immediately, sport educators engage the peer-leaders in the analysis of their teammates' game-play and identification of emerging tactical problems and errors. Sport educators discuss possible information that peer-leaders should provide to their teammates, they model potential forms of instruction (demonstration, explanation, questioning), and encourage the peer-leaders to help their teammates next time this problem occurs.

Box 3.9 Task: guided observation and the task structure/ scaffolding alignment

The integration of the peer-coach role and the use of guided practice implies that the task structure is designed in line with this intention. For example, allowing the regular rotation of the role of players and observers, grouping learners in teams of seven players to play a 3v3 game leaves one learner out in turns to provide peer feedback.

Guided task presentation

Guided task presentation is useful when learners already have some experience in leading instructional processes. The goal is that learners become less directive during the task presentation to their peers. Sport educators can try to get peer-coaches to explain the relationships between the tasks presented and the game problems they intend to solve.

Typically, the educators will assist or model the peer-coaches' task presentation by providing cues that fill in gaps in their instruction. They may also help them follow through a particular sequence of more democratic instruction (e.g., "start with the general aim, then show the full task, and finish up by repeating the two critical components").

Corner's meeting

The corner's meeting is an interactive management strategy (preparing the next activity while the current one is going on) for avoiding breaking the game practice of all learners. The selected leading learners quickly assemble with the educator to set up the next task and the expectations for their intervention (who is presenting the task, who is providing feedback). In case they need additional support, peer-coaches can request a corner's meeting from the educator any time during the task.

Reflective group discussions

Recently, Godbout et al. (2020, pp. 437–438) briefly illustrated the notion of reflective group discussion as a debate-of-ideas that can be defined as a

> learning set-up in which students express themselves and exchanges facts, opinions, reflections, and hypotheses concerning prior and coming game play. Once informed of their teammate's observations (augmented feedback), students undertake a discussion intended to elaborate strategies for the coming play practice.

From a scaffolding perspective, sport educators can promote group discussions as a context for mediating learners' collaborative identification of game problems and setting of following game-play or task design action.

Box 3.10 Task: scaffolding group discussions

In an initial stage of the learner-oriented experience, sport educators can mediate the group evaluation, planning, and monitoring of plans of action. They may help learners solve cognitive conflicts, by exploring the limits of their proposals, guide learners to consider how the proposed solutions would solve the problem and to anticipate any difficulties the solutions might pose, prompt them to explain and justify their own positions, and recognize uncertainties about and evaluate various perspectives and importance of the selected solutions.

In a more advanced stage of the learner-oriented experience, the educator may invest in supporting learners to become themselves the facilitators of the instructional and social interactions. Learners can be trained to ask thought-provoking questions, receive procedural guidance on the types of questions that will engage them in different problem-solving steps, demonstrations can be made of the question-generation process, or the educator can facilitate group members to practice asking each other various types of questions on a given problem scenario.

Box 3.11 Key point: guided observation and collaborative problem-solving

The guided observation strategy (Box 3.9) can also be applied during group discussions. The full team is engaged in video-based analysis of their game-play in the form of debate-of-ideas or in the observation of opponent teams.

Contingency: fitting the scaffolding to the situation

The principle of "instruction economy" (Rink, 2020) is a strong ingredient in successful teaching and coaching. It seeks to promote the expected responses in learners with the least amount of instructional time spent. If an educator can have learners on-task after a 30-seconds verbal instruction, it will be inappropriate to spent 5 minutes providing a complete demonstration of that task.

In addition, there are several contextual factors that sport educators need to consider during the selection of scaffolding strategies. The same scaffolding strategy may work differently for different learners who have different learning styles[4] or ability levels (Wibowo & Dyson, 2021). Consider the following instruction (basketball): "watch out for that dribbling". This cue can be sufficient or even stimulating for higher-skilled learners who can self-regulate and change their performance accordingly by drawing on their current skills. The absence of explicit information can lead learners to self-analyse the specific aspects that are hindering their performance, helping them to reach a better comprehension of the links between the motor components of that skill (e.g., keep head-up during dribbling, follow-the-ball-through using the wrist) and its efficient execution.

Conversely, this instruction may be completely useless for lower-skilled learners who may need more explicit information. They won't be able to self-regulate or figure out what might be wrong in their dribbling on their own.

Therefore, contingency is about making sure there is a *situation-intervention alignment*. The educators should consider different aspects in the contingent use of scaffolding.

The context of the activity (practice/competition)

It is important to note the *immediacy* component of any instructional intervention and to consider the temporal scope of learners' expected responses. Especially in the context of coaching, instruction takes place in different moments of the training context (introductory, main, and final part of the session) or in the context of competition (in-action, timeout, or recess). For example, in the introductory part of practice, there may be more room for using more implicit instructions (whiteboard, task cards). In the fundamental part, priority can be given to discovery-based instruction (cues, game modification) to deepen the understanding of the most complex tasks. The session ends with questioning prompts in group processing sessions ("What did we want to develop today? What do we need to improve next?").

During timeout competition moments, sport educators need to guide learners to a quick understanding of the situation and to point out to certain appropriate motor responses through simplified cues and questions. During game-play action, more immediate learner responses are requested. Explicit instruction will likely be more effective.

The complexity and progression of the subject-matter content

The level and nature of the scaffolding should be adjusted to the complexity of the game-based content being introduced. Learners may need more explicit support when presented with new tactical problems. Imagine an educator who wishes to lead on players to find a cross movement as a new means for the left-wingers and the right backcourt to create space and scoring in 2v2 situations. It might make sense to build this new ability on top of a game task (5v5) used previously to create space through a lower-complex tactics; attacking the even-odd opponent.

Learners' (and sport educators') level of previous performance, experience, and familiarity with the specific content and teaching-learning process

The million-dollar question in a learner-oriented approach is, "can learners build this new skill upon their prior knowledge and experiences?" As highlighted in the basketball dribbling example, the relevance of the instruction provided by a sport educator will depend on the current developmental stage of each learner.

This is also true for the sport educator. A common pitfall when sport educators try to transfer decision-making responsibility to learners is to blind-leap into using strategies that they do not master. So, it is critical that the educator self-regulates his own ability to successfully apply the selected scaffolding. Early and careful planning of the instruction intervention ("Where am I going to position myself on the court?" "When do I call a corner's meeting?" "What do I do when learners start presenting the task?") is important for successful teaching and coaching.

Progressive transfer of responsibility to learners

Sport educators may find helpful to frame the growing level of decision-making responsibility transferred to learners in reference to specific teaching or coaching instructional processes. Namely, planning (content selection, task design), implementing (content delivery: task presentation, in-task intervention), and assessing (feedback and monitoring of learner performance; Farias et al., 2018).

During the teaching-learning process, the nature and timing of the scaffolding evolve in close alignment with the level of responsibility that sport educators intend to transfer to learners. Table 3.3 (*Progressive levels of instructional responsibility: Task selection and presentation*) provides one example of the progressive and gradual engagement of learners in instructional processes of increasing complexity.

Table 3.3 Progressive levels of instructional responsibility: task selection and presentation

Instructional process: Task selection and presentation

Role and Responsibility level		Scaffolding
Level 3 Educator	Provides indirect teaching resources (task cards, video-tasks, etc.), offering varied tactical tasks and content of increasing complexity.	Indirect instruction: builds indirect teaching resources in advance (task cards, video-tasks, etc.). Post-lesson briefing: in the previous training, the educator provides teaching resources to peer-coaches and anticipates the expectations on their engagement in the process. The educator scaffolds different task content possibilities upon prior practice contexts ("task x, for example, very similar to the 5v5 we worked on yesterday, but this time the support on the sides helps playing wider").
Learner	Homework study of the tasks, selects and presents appropriate tactical tasks. Should prepare arguments to justify the link between intended content and task design.	Pre-lesson briefing: the peer-coaches test their tasks with the educator.

Instructional process: Task selection and presentation

Role and Responsibility level			Scaffolding
Level 2	Educator	Identify game problems, select learning content, and design the tasks.	Pre-lesson briefing: educator demonstrates the task solely to peer-coaches who are engaged in experimenting and demonstrating the task, stressing its critical points.
	Learner	Leads task presentation for introducing the content to their peers (content delivery).	Guided task presentation: educator provides support during learners' task presentation.
Level 1	Educator	Identify game problems, select learning content, design, and present the task to introduce the sport content to the whole class/team.	Pre-lesson briefing: before practice the educator works with the peer-leaders selected for that session providing simplified instructional cues (how they should position during task presentation, voice inflexions, eye-contact, etc.).
	Learner	Leads repetition of the task presentation to their teammates.	Guided practice: Educator demonstrates the task to the whole class, explicitly indicates the motor skills that practitioners should perform and explain how they solve specific game problems. Peer-coaches are engaged in the guided practice demonstration.

Self-processing questions

Box 3.12 A time to reflect – content review

- Analyse Table 3.2 and locate your predominant teaching or coaching practice in the explicitness continuum. Are you happy about your conclusions? If not/yes, what now?
- Write down the scaffolding settings that you usually use in your professional practice, listing those that you are not using yet but intend to use in a new future.
- Reflect on the extent to which you can apply a plan of gradual transfer of responsibility to learners.

Summary and key points

This chapter explained what scaffolding is and its importance for helping sport educators to become successful facilitators in learners' sport development. Sport educators can apply a wide range of more explicit or more implicit scaffolding means (from demonstrations to exploring-based contexts) to encourage different levels of learners' involvement in building their learning experience. Contingency is a core feature of scaffolding, and sport educators should select their scaffolding strategies according to several contextual factors (e.g., the level of complexity of the learning content or learners' developmental stage). Finally, the coherent use of scaffolding can successfully sustain the gradual transfer of instructional responsibility to learners.

Notes

1 Scaffolding represents temporary pedagogical structures that explain the mediation role (supporting, steering, mediating, facilitating) that a sport educator, or a more experienced and knowledgeable sport learner, can play in joint problem-solving activities between sport educators and sport learners, or between sport learners themselves.
2 Note how the unfolding and content of the scaffolding instruction remains similar even though the sport is different (invasion, net, and striking/batting games).
3 For example, identifying personal and collective learning needs, monitoring, and assessing their own and their peers' practice and, selecting, or designing adult-designed or designing themselves appropriate tasks for solving personally relevant game problems.
4 Take a closer look to Godbout and Gréhaigne (2020) for insight on the location of learners' learning styles in dependency/independency self-regulation continuum.

References

Farias, C., Hastie, P., & Mesquita, I. (2018). Scaffolding student–coaches' instructional leadership toward student-centred peer interactions: A year-long action-research intervention in sport education. *European Physical Education Review, 24*(3), 269–291.

Godbout, P., & Gréhaigne, J. F. (2020). Regulation of tactical learning in team sports – the case of the tactical-decision learning model. *Physical Education and Sport Pedagogy.* DOI: 10.1080/17408989.2020.1861232

Hastie, P., & Mesquita, I. (2016). Sport-based physical education. In C. Ennis (Ed.), *Routledge handbook of physical education pedagogies* (pp. 367–379). London: Routledge.

King, A. (1992). Facilitating elaborative learning through guided student-generated questioning. *Educational Psychologist, 27*, 111–126.

Rink, J. E. (2020). *Teaching physical education for learning (8th edition).* Boston, MA: McGraw Hill Education.

Smit, J., van Eerde, H., & Bakker, A. (2013). A conceptualisation of whole-class scaffolding. *British Educational Research Journal, 39*, 817–834.

Van de Pol, J., Volman, M., & Beishuizen, J. (2010). Scaffolding in teacher–student interaction: A decade of research. *Educational Psychology Review, 22*(3), 271–296.

Vygotsky, L. S. (1978). *Mind in Society: The development of higher psychological processes.* Massachusetts: Harvard University Press.

Wibowo, J., & Dyson, B. (2021). A contingency perspective on learning and instruction in physical education. *European Physical Education Review, 27*(4), 727–742.

Xun, G. E., & Land, S. M. (2004). A conceptual framework for scaffolding III-structured problem-solving processes using question prompts and peer interactions. *Educational Technology Research and Development, 52*(2), 5–22.

4 Strategies for the Gradual Instructional Mediation of Learner-Oriented Interactions

Cláudio Farias, Tristan L. Wallhead and Isabel Mesquita

Box 4.1 Objectives

At the end of this chapter you will know how to:

- Establish student expectations for the foundation of peer-mediated learner-oriented interactions
- Use guided practice to model peer-coaches' solutions to game-play problems
- Use guided discussion to transition peer-coaches to become game problem-solvers
- Use group discussion to promote more discovery-based learning
- Use reflection prompts to empower all learners to take an active role in their own and others' construction of knowledge.

Box 4.2 Key sections

- Introduction
- Sport Educator mediated instructional interactions
- Scaffolding collaborative learning interactions
- Scaffolding learner-mediated instructional interactions.

Introduction

Following the presentation of the general conceptual principles of the scaffolding framework in Chapter 3, Chapter 4 offers a practical proposal for the progressive scaffolding of learner-oriented instructional interactions. It is important to note that it is often beneficial for sport

DOI: 10.4324/9781003140016-6

educators to start slowly with their scaffolding strategies. Sport educators should progressively build a sustainable sense of confidence through the gradual transfer of responsibility to learners. This will allow them to have a greater sense of control over the process of sharing decision-making power with learners.

Perception of insecurity is often one of the main reasons why sport educators revert to more directive and traditional approaches to instruction (Goodyear & Dudley, 2005). Sport educators must engage in a process of professional identity (re)construction through the transformation of conceptions of teaching or coaching and respective pedagogical practices. This is what will make the difference between a short-lived attempt at changing teaching and coaching practices or sport educators achieving a more self-determined and resilient pursuit of a learner-oriented approach (Farias, Hastie, & Mesquita, 2018).

Please note that the goal of scaffolding is to sustain learners' growing independence from sport educators and learners' active participation in the teaching-learning process of sport and games. We are not advocating that the three levels of scaffolding presented in this proposal should be applied in a "linear fashion".[1]

Instead, we are saying that the use of different levels of scaffolding by sport educators should progress as they feel increasingly confident about the understanding and mastery of the scaffolding process as a whole. Thus, the level of scaffolding applied should be informed by sport educators' current level of experience in the application of learner-oriented pedagogies, or by their ambition to progress to a higher level in involving learners actively in the learning process. Sport educators will also need to consider the developmental stage of the learners, that is, where they sit in their learner-oriented experience and ability to undertake responsibility.

For example, experienced sport educators can already start by scaffolding collaborative interactions between learners through group debate for identification of game problems and solutions (Wibowo & Dyson, 2021). Sport educators can also use this same scaffolding strategy in the next level of learners' engagement whereby a group of learners can be collaboratively trained to develop their peer-coaching skills to become themselves the main mediators of their teammates' learning (Mitchell, Oslin, & Griffin, 2020). Conversely, sport educators can feel more confident if they start by applying scaffolding strategies for the whole group, thus maintaining a more direct control of the pacing of most instructional interactions.

In agreement, we present a scaffolding proposal with three levels of mediation of instructional interactions: (1) scaffolding general instructional interactions; (2) scaffolding collaborative instructional interactions; and (3) scaffolding learner-led instructional interactions.

Scaffolding general instructional interactions

Especially in the early stages of scaffolding the learning of more complex sports content, it is likely that learners have an insufficient knowledge base or lack prior sport or game experiences on which to build the new knowledge.

It can be more productive for sport educators if they scaffold learners' discovery of game-play solutions and their building of game-play ability based upon a set of task goals and frame of problems set by sport educators. The scaffolding examples provided in this section involve general instructional interactions aimed mostly at learners' development as game-play performers.

Explanatory structures

In Box 4.3, a coach provides explanatory structures to justify the relevance of the task presented (Basketball: 3v2 game-based for creating space and attacking the basket). The scaffolding intervention links the features of the practice tasks to the game problems encountered during the main game form to spark a deeper understanding of the task content. Learners are expected to develop an initial understanding of how to learn games in a problem-solving fashion.

Box 4.3 Task: scaffolding – guided practice, explanatory structures

Educator: In the last match the off-the-ball players were great; they're cutting free of their markers and supporting, yet the defenders were still recovering ball possession mostly because you're overlapping each other and closing passing lanes. So, I've drawn some spots on the floor that will provide a reference where to run without overlapping each other. Watch. Anne and Joan, on each of the opposing spots please. Start moving slowly towards the ball. See the space getting open near the basket as Sarah "lures" the opponent out of position? Quick, cut back to the basket (v-cut). (*Sarah gets free, the ball is passed, and she scores*). Don't forget the target-hand to signal where you want the ball.

Discovery-based instruction (questioning and hints)

At an early stage in the development of any sports content, sport educators should expect to have a more active intervention in guiding learners towards the achievement of the task goals. In the following example (Box 4.4) the sport educator uses questioning and provides hints to help the learners understand and analyse the circumstances of their game actions (e.g., reading the content-embedded cues) to identify the relationship between the play situation and the appropriate game-play actions for improving the volleyball spike. The second part of the interaction exemplifies how the sport educator can begin to scaffold the discovery of new solutions (new learning content) to this game situation.

**Box 4.4 Task: scaffolding in-task intervention –
questioning and hints**

(CONVERGENT SCAFFOLDING)
EDUCATOR: Stop! Laura, what just happened?
LAURA: Hmmm ... I spiked out of bounds...?
EDUCATOR: Yes, but why did that happen?
LAURA: I don't know...
EDUCATOR: Would there be a more appropriate jumping point?
How far were you from the net?
LAURA: Maybe I wasn't well positioned for attacking the ball...?
EDUCATOR: I think so. Where did you attack the ball? Did you
notice?
LAURA: Yes, I was too far from the ball contact point! I was already descending when I reached the hitting spot.
EDUCATOR: What can you do to change that?
LAURA: I think, starting the run-up closer to the net.
EDUCATOR: So, let's try again and see what happens.
...
(DIVERGENT SCAFFOLDING)
EDUCATOR: Now, what if the other team defends in a
double-block format? What implications does this have
for where you spike? What if your setter stays too far down
court? What if the other team plays in a 3:1 system? What
then...? Show me how you and your teammates would position themselves.

Structural-based scaffolding

Sport educators may also use basic structural elements of the teaching-learning process as a scaffolding tool that entails less explicit instruction intervention. This structural scaffolding may include the *manipulation of learning task conditions* (see Chapter 7) to scaffold learners' *transfer of game-play skills across different games or learning tasks*.

To facilitate the transfer of learners' knowledge across different sport content, sport educators can design a sequential development of content in reference to different game forms within a same game category (e.g., invasion games).[2]

Preserving task conditions such as field width and length, goalkeeper area, and attack/defense player ratio across different games has the potential to present the same configuration of problems for learners to solve. This can be an effective means for prompting new sport-specific knowledge. It also facilitates learners' transfer of problem-solving skills across similar, but still differentiated games, which calls for the "natural" emergence and application of similar tactical solutions. It also leaves room for the improvement of sport-specific skills as the practice of that specific game form progresses.

Figure 4.1 provides an example of content development using "structural" scaffolding across indoor handball-, football-, or hockey-based

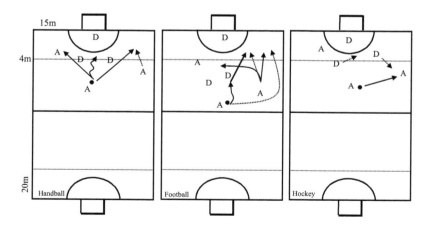

Notes: attackers (A); defenders (D)
Legend: ●ball; ⟶ pass; ⌇▲dribble; ┈┈▶ off-the-ball move.

Figure 4.1 Content development "structural" scaffolding across indoor handball-, football-, and field hockey-based games.

games which preserves similar task conditions. The three game forms have a similar structure where there is numerical superiority whenever the team is in attack. The examples of handball and football portray offensive tactical moves commonly used by learners to solve situations related to the use and creation of space in situations of numerical superiority (i.e., opening wide, 2v1 fixing the defending before passing, passing, fast breaking and overlapping, passing across opposite court lanes, etc.). Defensive moves common to all three situations are portrayed in hockey. When in a defensive process (and in numerical inferiority), defenders need to occupy the space with constant coordinated movements of interception attempts and respective covering by the second defender. Sport educators can refine their ability to use structural scaffolding in Chapter 7.

Scaffolding collaborative interactions

Following the organisation of learners into persistent learning teams and when the scaffolding of the learners' active involvement in the activities is already a habitual routine in the sport educator's instruction, it is time to invest in scaffolding strategies that will improve learners' ability to share knowledge and collaborate towards improved problem-solving. In this phase of the learner-oriented experience, learners can be prepared to be the main identifiers of the most relevant problems in their practice, establish their own learning objectives, and design their own task solutions (see Chapter 8).

Scaffolding group debate and collaborative problem-solving

The collaborative construction of learning experiences should be informed by sport educators' in-depth knowledge of the strengths and limitations of each learner in the group. The following example (Box 4.5) shows how gaps in learners' game understanding can be filled in by their peers. At this point, sport educators and learners should already be confident about the process of responsibility transfer, and thus, interactions can be built in reference to game problems identified by the learners themselves. The learners are engaged in a *group discussion* about a game-based field hockey task, which highlights a collaborative problem-solving situation based on *video observation of tactical problems* (creating/using/defending space). In addition, Box 4.6 shows how to scaffold learners' design of tasks as a more complex property of the problem-solving process.

Box 4.5 Task: scaffolding – pre-lesson briefing; guided observation and group discussion for collaborative problem-solving and learning

EDUCATOR: What were the main offensive problems you had in the last game-play session?

ROSE: The wing guys are standing too close. At other times they're already deep down to the goal.

CHRIS: Plus, they're passing too soon. One defender has time to tackle two attackers.

EDUCATOR: Okay, let's watch a series of your teams' attack plays.

(THE VIDEO IS SET TO RUN)

EDUCATOR: What's happening here and why?

ROSE: I always need to be calling "come back".

EDUCATOR: Right, but that concerns an individual! What about the specific moment your players step in for a 2v1 attack? What's wrong there?

(SILENCE)

EDUCATOR: Lisa, can you help the guys here?

LISA: It's too risky to pass from side-lane to side-lane.

CHRIS: I noticed that Karen and John do that a lot. Still, if one defender is outwitted...

JOHN: You cannot place one player forward and another covering.

EDUCATOR: John, can you elaborate further on that?

JOHN: When the attacker passes the ball to the side-lane and then cuts....

LISA: Ah! In this sense she takes advantage of the open space.

The previous example showed how to help learners solve problems through different "discrete" and random game actions. At the next stage of the learners' active participation in the learning process, they can be encouraged to engage in group discussion for building more elaborate solutions to problems. The following example (Box 4.6) shows how to scaffold goal-setting and the respective construction of learning tasks as led by learners. The sport educator can scaffold the building of the new tasks on top of learners' prior experiences of participation in similar learning tasks.

Box 4.6 Task: scaffolding – pre-lesson briefing; guided task structure for mediating goal-setting and learner-led task design

EDUCATOR: What problems will you be working on in today's basketball session?

SARAH: We have low mobility in the attack, we don't attack the open space.

EDUCATOR: How can you work on that?

SARAH: Find ways to have them pass, cut, pass, and then shoot.

EDUCATOR: Paul, go back to that 3v1 game you presented last week. The side-lanes were bounded to one player. What came out of that?

PAUL: They were able to get wide open more easily.

EDUCATOR: Now, how can we transfer that principle to the new task? What space needs to be open now?

SARAH: In the centre-lane, right between the 6- and the 9-meter lines. We could set an off-limit square. The attackers will have more time to rotate and shoot.

EDUCATOR: Okay, let's test the task before the session starts and see how it goes...

Scaffolding the pacing of collaborative interactions

An additional scaffolding strategy of collaborative interactions may involve setting the *pacing of the instruction interventions*. Sport educators can define the exact *timing* (e.g., during the transition between task A and B) of *learners' engagement in group discussion*. Put simply, reflective group debates are integrated into the pacing of tasks progression.[3]

At an early stage, sport educators may need to be more explicit in the focus and exact timing of the group discussion interactions taking place. Later, learners can be encouraged to select (and justify) their own timing and problem-solving goals.

The following example in softball (Box 4.7) channels the learners' attention to preventing scoring situations and is directed at supporting players in a 0–1 out, runner on first game situation. The task is designed to elicit problem situations arising during a 4v4 small-sided game when players struggle to determine the best position for base coverage or deciding where to position for backup. The sport educator tries to establish a link between the new and prior learning content and steers the learners' attention to specific elements of the game and pacing of instructional interactions.

Box 4.7 Task: structural scaffolding – timing the pacing of instruction

EDUCATOR: Last week we worked on our batting and running scoring moves from first to second bases. Why were we so successful in that 4v4 game? Think of the infielders.

PETE: We lacked coordination in throwing between bases.

EDUCATOR: Yes, that was one of the main issues. But there are several details in these moves that influenced that outcome (e.g., the infielders, throwing and receiving were not getting in the same side of the base runner, and many throws hitting the runners).

Now you will play two 15-minute games. In the first game simply play the game, freely. Yet, you'll mentally record the first to second base defensive errors as you play. When you finish the game, you will have 5 minutes to discuss these issues and draw up action plans. In the second 15-minute game you will test those moves. You may interrupt the game whenever you want to adjust and try out new moves.

Note: depending on the team/class size and the number of players per team, a learner can be assigned to analyse and assess their teammates' behaviour. In the second game block, learners can rotate in the role of peer-observer/assesser.

Scaffolding learner-led instructional interactions

Scaffolding basic peer-coaching instructional skills

When sport educators wish that a significant part of the learning of sport and games takes place through peer-coaching dynamics, that necessarily implies a redefinition of the scaffolding strategies. Peer-leaders must be progressively prepared to become (pro)active mediators of their own sport development and that of their peers.

However, sport learners are typically concerned with their own game-play and do not often convey a predisposition to pay attention to their peers' performance and provide evaluative feedback. Thus, at an early stage of the implementation of peer-coaching dynamics the scaffolding should focus on making learners aware of the responsibility and expectations inherent in performing peer-coaching roles (e.g., helping their peers to learn games).

Box 4.8   Key point: learners should not be overwhelmed by peer-teaching duties

A balance should be established between peer-coaching duties and peer-coaches' achievement of their personal expectations about game-play participation and performance improvement. As learners progress in their peer-coaching they will become increasingly motivated for contributing to their peers' game-play development.

The responsibility transferred to peer-coaches may focus initially on the presentation of tasks involving less complex content (with less contextual interference such as game-related technical skills) and repetition of more complex tasks previously presented by the sport educator.

An initial step in this process may be the *scaffolding of basic peer-coaching instructional skills and strategies* (Box 4.9).

Box 4.9   Task: scaffolding – guided practice; modelling basic peer-coaching instructional strategies

TEACHER: This is not new to the class, so, coaches, watch how I use minimal instruction to explain the goal of the task and quickly organise where the players should position.

WHOLE CLASS INSTRUCTION: "Two attackers you start on that line spread apart. Attackers, you are trying to get passed the defender and score by dribbling the ball over the far line at the other end of the grid. Defenders you are in the middle of the grid. Defender starts with the ball and passes to one of the attackers, as soon as this occurs, they can defend and try and steal the ball."

PEER-COACHING MODELLING: "Now, before you instruct, make sure everybody is watching, keep the eye contact while talking. Note how I place myself to provide a correct demonstration of what I want them to do. First, I demonstrate the attack moves, then I repeat for the defensive moves. Now, before starting, make sure they give it a go, you can even allow a slow motion first trial."

WHOLE CLASS INSTRUCTION: "Ready, go..."

Scaffolding peer-coaching's use of question-asking skills

Not surprisingly, most peer-coaches tend to be very directive with their peers. As the learner-oriented experience progresses, sport educators should make increasing efforts to turn peer-coaches into their "assistant coaches" to promote the more active engagement of all learners in building their experience of learning (about and) how to be better game-players. Make no mistake, if learner-oriented interactions are to happen during peer-teaching activities, then peer-coaches will have to develop some level of basic instructional skills to make this happen.

Box 4.10 Key point: learner-oriented peer-coaching requires training

In a learner-oriented approach learners are not supposed to have the same instructional skills as a teacher or a coach. Yet, they are expected to play a more active role in instructional processes to the extent that it is reasonable to ask, for example, of a young student or athlete. So that the instructional interactions led by the learners themselves are not entirely based on the direct transmission of content by peer-coaches with low cognitive involvement of their mates, sport educators must train these learners to use (simplified) less explicit instructional strategies.

Within this journey, sport educators can *encourage peer-coaches to use less explicit "lines of instruction"*. The goal is for learners to be able to participate in cognitive processing and understanding of content even when they are taught by their peers. The following example (Box 4.11) shows how sport educators can *model the use of question-asking instruction* to a group of peer-coaches.[4]

Box 4.11 Task: scaffolding – pre-lesson briefing; guided task presentation/group discussion, modelling question-asking skills and collaborative reflection

EDUCATOR: "Stop." freeze like a statue, "Mary, move over here. Why did you lose the ball?" Instead of simply telling her "open wide," what question would lead her to understand why she needs to open wide?

PETER: "What do you need to do to catch the ball away from the defender?"

EDUCATOR: Great question. How do you think she would answer?

CHRIS: They'd need to move to the side-lines to get free from defence.

....

EDUCATOR: How are you planning your intervention today and why?

REBECCA: I think it's probably better the way Laura is doing it. She explains the movements while they're playing the first game and in the second game she can check if they are learning better and then leaves them to free play.

GUY: We can also observe the errors first, wait until they happen, and then explain.

EDUCATOR: Why are you using this strategy?

LAURA: I'm slowing the game pace and trying to explain while they test different tactics. Then, go back to regular game-play for a while.

A very effective strategy is also the promotion of debates among peer-coaches such that they can challenge each other's thinking, construct arguments, and justify their use of particular instructional strategies in the development of their teams' game-play skills.

Scaffolding peer-coaching use of scaffolding strategies

Though we acknowledge this is quite ambitious (but we also assure you this is feasible), sport educators can train peer-coaches to *scaffold their peers' learning of new knowledge based upon their prior learning experiences*. The following example (Box 4.12) shows how peer-coaches can be guided to prompt teammates to use past game solutions and knowledge to solve current tactical problems. After noticing how difficult it is for coaches to identify ways of scaffolding their teammates' handball game-play, the sport educator brings together the group of peer-coaches to engage them in a moment of *guided observation* of their teammates' game-play.

Box 4.12 Task: scaffolding – coaches corner's meeting; guided observation/group discussion; modelling peer-coaching's use of scaffolding strategies

EDUCATOR: How could you go back to basketball and get something that could have helped them understand what they were doing wrong here?

RITA: That move, stopping and waiting for support?

EDUCATOR: Every time you made that initial give-and-go, what got open?

SEVERAL: Space near the basket.

EDUCATOR: Is it that different now (in handball)?

MIKE: No, it's the same, but now we have a goal not a basket.

EDUCATOR: So, why not use their knowledge from basketball, "remember basketball when the defense left the space at their back?" or use your own knowledge, for example from football, "the faults are alike now, the game restarts at the exact spot."

LISA: We can go back to those things they did great before so that they remember and do it now.

Self-processing Questions

Box 4.13 A time to reflect – content review

- Think back to your last few weeks of teaching or coaching practice and reflect on the extent to which you are using learner-oriented scaffolding strategies.
- On that basis, write up what you are going to do in your next practice (introduce new scaffolding strategies, reinforce the use of current scaffolding strategies, etc.).
- Use one of the scaffolding examples (e.g., video-based group discussion about tactical problems), plan an instructional sequence (e.g., questioning), and engage your learners in that sequence.
- Reflect on the extent to which the learners' responses aligned with your expectations and what you might need to do to improve this process.

Summary and key points

This chapter presented several strategies for the progressive scaffolding of learners' active engagement in the learning (and peer-teaching) of sport and games. Two levels of instructional interactions were scaffolded: interactions that occur between the sport educator and the main group of students, and interactions that occur among the learners themselves (both in collaborative and peer-coaching activities). The first level of mediation interaction can include the scaffolding of learners' understanding of how to learn about games in a problem-solving logic and become more proficient in the identification of relevant game problems and respective solutions. At the second interactional level, sport educators can scaffold learners' co-construction of learning and employ implicit structural interactions (manipulation of task conditions and content development sequences). Finally, sport educators can prepare peer-coaches for assuming responsibility for the mediation of their teammates' active engagement in the learning experience. This included the training of basic instructional skills, question-asking ability, and the scaffolding of their teammates' learning.

Notes

1 In fact, this can negate the very essence of scaffolding and the contingency principle (see Chapter 3).
2 This is a foundational premise of several game-based approaches (see Mitchell, Oslin, & Griffin, 2020). In the present book, the content development choices a sport educator makes can act, per se, as a scaffold that facilitates learners' transfer of game-play skills and understanding across different practice contexts. The same is true for promoting the transfer of knowledge across tasks related to the same game.
3 The *reflective group debate* notion we propose here may resonate strongly with the debate-of-ideas concept presented by Godbout and Gréhaigne (2020). Sport educator should note that in Godbout and Gréhaigne (2020), the debate of ideas is integrated in a methodological sequence that is somewhat more delimited and linear. In the present proposal we suggest sport educators should focus on the group discussion component, with consequent identification of problems and setting of subsequent plans of action. This can include either operationalizing in the following game practice a given strategic plan or specific tactical moves or designing a new practice task to work on these issues (see Group debate for collaborative identification of problems and co-construction of solutions).
4 The sport educator can group several peer-coaches and work aside with that persistent bunch for several weeks. The collaborative premises

proposed in "Scaffolding collaborative learning activities" can well be used for improving their peer-coaching skills.

References

Farias, C., Hastie, P., & Mesquita, I. (2018). Scaffolding student–coaches' instructional leadership toward student-centred peer interactions: A year-long action-research intervention in sport education. *European Physical Education Review, 24*, 269–291. doi: 10.1177/1356336X16687303

Godbout, P., & Gréhaigne, J. F. (2020). Revisiting the tactical-decision learning model. *Quest, 72*(4), 430–447.

Goodyear, V., & Dudley, D. (2015). I'm a facilitator of learning! Understanding what teachers and students do within student-centered physical education models. *Quest, 67*(3), 274–289.

Mitchell, S. A., Oslin, J., & Griffin, L. L. (2020). *Teaching sport concepts and skills: A tactical games approach*. Champaign, IL: Human Kinetics.

Wallhead, T. L. (2017). Developing student coaches in the Sport Education model. *ACHPER Active and Healthy Journal, 24*, 21–24.

Wibowo, J., & Dyson, B. (2021). A contingency perspective on learning and instruction in Physical Education. *European Physical Education Review*. doi: 1356336X20985884

5 Strategies for Mediating Democratic, Meaningful, and Collaborative Learning Environments

Engaging Sport Educators and Sport Learners as Transforming Social Agents

Cláudio Farias and Isabel Mesquita

Box 5.1 Objectives

At the end of this chapter you will be able to:

- Scaffold quality social interactions between learners.
- Use different scaffolding strategies (structural, contextual, and peer-mediation) for promoting the democratic and meaningful participation of learners in sport and games.

Box 5.2 Key sections

- Introduction
- Social development and positive interactions as the active promotion of more democratic, fair, empathetic, and equitable learning contexts
- Scaffolding positive social interactions
- Structural-based Scaffolding
- Contextual-based scaffolding
- Scaffolding learner-mediated social interactions

DOI: 10.4324/9781003140016-7

Introduction

Many of the instructional interactions necessary to implement a learner-oriented approach to teaching and learning sport and games depend on peer-coaching dynamics, positive collaboration, and productive knowledge exchange between learners. Since any instructional process is simultaneously a social interaction (influenced by who we are as human beings), the quality of social interactions will necessarily affect the quality of any instructional interaction. Therefore, to take care of the quality of instruction, sport educators must take care first, or at least concurrently and in equal proportion, of the quality of learners' socialization. Facilitating the construction of healthy social interactions between learners is a central concern of sport educators.

In this perspective, scaffolding also becomes a between-people mediation tool through which sport educators support learners' learning and social development through the relationships that they establish with learners and between learners. Scaffolding is also critical for developing positive shared beliefs and knowledge interactions between learners so that they understand and accept each other as unique learners, social, and human beings.

While Chapter 4 offered a scaffolding framework for the gradual support of the active participation of learners in the instructional construction of their sporting experience, this chapter offers scaffolding strategies for the personal and social development of learners while they develop as a community of learners.

It can be said that the scaffolding processes offered here represent a growing challenge for sport educators, but they also support their growing ability to manage increasingly sophisticated social mediation processes. The following sections show how sport educators can use instructional (e.g., task structure) and contextual (e.g., student accountability systems) social scaffolding strategies. Next, sport educators are guided on how to involve the learners themselves as "active agents" in the mediation of their social interactions.

Positive social development and interactions: the active development of more democratic, empathetic, and equitable learning contexts

Social development and learners' participation in meaningful sport-based experiences can be expressed when learners progress in showing care, concern, empathy, respect for each other, actively supporting and encouraging one another to learn (Beni, Fletcher, & Ní Chróinín, 2017).

Box 5.3 Key point: positive learning environments

In a positive learning environment, meaningful experiences arise when both sport educators and learners are empowered to actively act as agents of social change and are offered the opportunity to appreciate the value of inclusion, equity, and building of responsible leadership and empathetic teamwork skills.

However, the development of collaborative and positive social interactions between learners does not spontaneously emerge from simply grouping children in persistent teams and getting them to play together. On the contrary, when learners are given power to manage their sporting interactions and experiences, and this process is not properly scaffolded, negative *contextual, relational*, or *structural* influences may emerge. Typically, less "dominant" learners may come to have a lower participation in the learning activities.

Sport educators should take proper precautions about the following:

– There can be cases of unequal decision-making hierarchies and discriminatory use of power exhibited by learners who assume leadership of game-play activities (usually higher-skilled learners with a strong background in community-based sport).
– The teams often establish the level of participation in the activities based on learners' sex, popularity, or skill-level ("most popular and higher-ability learners decide who plays and who stays out").
– There are some hegemonic discourses of masculinity that both teachers and learners perpetuate in their PE lessons or youth sport contexts ("girls are not aggressive sport-players").
– Some deep-rooted misconceptions on sporting expectations related to gendered stereotypes may be pervasive ("girls can't play sports").
– Negative social interactions may arise when teachers place an excessive emphasis on competition events, or when there is a lack of balance between learners' opportunities to participate in team practice games and the provision of a "just right" amount of participation in competition events.

The scaffolding strategies presented below are grounded on evidence collected from practical contexts in physical education (PE) and youth sport teams. The scaffolding processes include: "Scaffolding positive social interactions"; "Structural-based Scaffolding"; "Contextual-based scaffolding"; and "Scaffolding learner-mediated social interactions".

Scaffolding positive social interactions

Sports panel and group discussions

In any sporting context, interactions taking place between people necessarily develop in reference to a set of expectations regarding what are the behaviours or attitudes that someone who belongs to that community should show. Any breaches occurring in the social conduct agreed by the larger group can be dealt with within a "**sports panel**". Several learners can be made representatives, for example, of their learning teams.[1] Please note that the dynamics taking place in this setting can take the form of focused "**social-oriented group discussions**". These reflective debates can be extended to any specific subgroup of learners on which a more individualized intervention is needed to improve less positive social interactions occurring between them. Sport educators can also rotate the participation of all learners through the sports panel. Specific periods of time may be allocated for these meetings before or after the sessions (pre/post-session briefings).

The goal is to scaffold learners' reflection about the impact of their actions on others to promote the collective construction of positive ways of being and belonging to that community of learners (e.g., how the class conceives of inclusiveness and its implications to the way individual playing time is to be set within the team). Multiple topics can be explored in these group discussions:

- Breaking down stereotyped, discriminatory, and bullying behaviours.
- Implement empathy development exercises: "put yourself in the other's shoes".
- Renegotiate rules of group conduct, prompting awareness of the need to display inclusive attitudes, and promote equity participation among learners.
- Prompt the emergence of learners' embodied sense of caring for others and sharing of individual knowledge repertoires with less skilful peers.

Sport educators' scaffolding of positive social interactions can occur during in-task interventions (e.g., stopping game-play practice and stepping in to engage learners in reflective discussion on social justice situations). In addition, when sport educators notice the recurrent emergence of negative social interactions, they can selectively collect video images of particular practice events to engage learners in the analysis of those situations.

Box 5.4 Key point: benefits of scaffolding positive and inclusive social interactions

- It locates the negotiation of conflicts at the micro-level of peer interactions, fading the more pronounced teacher-learner hierarchical asymmetry often present in more teacher/ coach-centred learning contexts.
- Learners are intrinsically prompted to deal with the consequences of their actions in accordance with the rules they have established.
- The systematic reflection on the accomplishment of the ethical contract's goals provides the opportunity to constantly revisit conceptions of equity and progression in their levels of responsibility.

The following task (Box 5.5) depicts a recurrent situation in any given context involving the practice of sport by young people. The sport educator steers a possible line of group reflection to "deconstruct" potential misrepresentations (often of cultural origin) that tend to wrongly influence the judgement that some learners make in relation to those responsible for the errors occurring during game-play.

Box 5.5 Task: scaffolding: in-task intervention or post-lesson video analysis; reflective questioning.

EDUCATOR: Stop, what just happened?
PETE: Mary made a bad pass to Gary and it went out of bounds.
EDUCATOR: Gary, what do you think?
GARY: I agree, Mary is not that good in long passing.
EDUCATOR: Hmmm. Mary, anyone else, do you agree?
MARY: The pass was too long but it was hard to pass, I don't think it is all my fault.
EDUCATOR: Right. Let's think about it for a while. A pass and a reception, what makes these two actions successful?
GARY: You need to pass within a catchable range.
EDUCATOR: That's right. What about the catcher. What's his role in the success of the passing?
PETE: He needs to move appropriately. The right distance and open.
EDUCATOR: Right. Now, watch the moment Mary is passing...

GARY: She's kind of blocked. The only chance is to make a rainbow pass. Which she did.

EDUCATOR: Basically, the only way this pass could be successful would be if...

PETE: The catcher needed to open more widely.

EDUCATOR: Actually, it seems she did a great pass then, a perfect rainbow trajectory...

GARY: Ah! I stood in that spot when I needed to be wide open. I guess my support move wasn't that good.

EDUCATOR: Yes, it is a team's game. Perhaps we can think twice before blaming someone. What could have helped here?

GARY: Perhaps, "well done Mary! Next time just wait a bit until I open wide".

Structural-based Scaffolding (attending to intra- and inter-individual variability)

The scaffolding of positive social interactions between learners can also take the form of more implicit interventions. This section shows how sport educators can apply specific task organization and content development dynamics to scaffold more democratic patterns of learner participation in the activities.

Aligning task conditions and group formation

The sport educator, or learners themselves, can be tasked to discuss and design equitable task rotation systems displayed as a "formal" schedule of participation in game-play activities. The following aligns content selection (e.g., game forms) with the formation of learning groups and learners' level of participation in the activities.

Box 5.6 Task: any game to be played in a 3-a-side format

Game form: 3v3
  Group work: 8 learners
  Game-play duration: 2 × 8-min games
  Player rotation: every 2-min

Note: This participation setting has the potential to promote equitable participation. Each learner will play for 12 minutes (game 1: 6-min; game 2: 6-min).

Inclusive manipulation of task conditions for
meeting different learning needs

Inclusion-driven sport educators, those who seek to respond to the unique personal characteristics of each learner, will try to consider the inter-individual differences of learners. For example, to prevent some learners (usually the lower-skilled ones) from feeling left out, sport educators must be able to design and modify games[2] that allow learners with different skill levels to successfully participate in the same activity.

The modification of the playing areas and game rules to match learners' ability level may include:

– Changing the scoring systems to facilitate equitable on-the-ball participation (three points awarded if all players touch the ball before a goal attempt).
– Establishing safety areas on the court where students can refine basic skills within the game (e.g., dribbling and passing), pass the ball safely, and gain confidence before engaging in more pressing game interactions against opponents.
– Individual adjustments applied to the level of defensive pressure (e.g., no interception allowed during players' dribbling for scoring).

The 3v3 basketball-based task presented below (Box 5.7) and respective Figure 5.1, create a context in which game skills of different complexity are required from learners with different skill levels. Importantly, both lower- and higher-skilled learners are challenged at an appropriate level.

Box 5.7 Task: an inclusive 3v3 game

Each team contains three learners with different skill levels (lowest: A1, D1; medium: A2, D2; and higher: A3, D3).

The player-to-player rule is used (each player faces a direct opponent of similar strength) and some rules are individually adapted to the level of each player:

A1, D1 – Interception is not allowed at any moment ("cold" defense).

A2, D2 – No interception allowed within the restricted area (3-second allowed to shoot at basket, "warm" defense).
A3, D3 – Interception is allowed at full-court ("hot" defense).

Notes: The rules dictate that each learner will have more/less time to think/execute and will be called upon to use motor skills consistent with their current ability level. For example, "hot" defense will require that A3, D3 frequently score through lay-up shots due to the close defensive pressure; A2, D2 can use short shots close to the basket, a less demanding skill than the lay-up shot; A1, D1 do not yet need to use protection dribbling to progress to the basket which provides them more time for keeping their heads up and reading the game. As learners evolve, the facilitating rules will be removed.

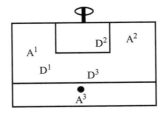

Figure 5.1 Inclusive task: including different game demands and learners of different skill levels in the same activity.
Notes: A: attackers; D: defenders.

Graded competition

In a learner-oriented approach much of learner development is driven by peer-teaching and collaborative learning interactions. Thus, the higher-skilled learners must also be challenged at an appropriate level as they are the ones who frequently lead the exchange of knowledge during collaborative interactions. Basically, higher-skilled learners should not feel that they are being "instrumentalized" by sports educators as "mere teaching tools and knowledge resources" at the "disposal" of their less-skilled mates.

However, it can be very difficult for sport educators to functionally integrate players of different skill levels in the same task when the differences between learners are too striking.[3] In some cases, the composition of heterogeneous teams can lead to a critical reduction in the level of challenge that the game poses to the most skilled learners with their consequent disengagement of the activity.

Yet, sport educators can form **sub-teams of different levels** within the same learning team, using some task modification premises suggested in the previous point.[4] As a complement, sport educators can promote **graded competition events.**[5] The concept of graded competition, for example, forming two "competition divisions" (Division A; Division B) provides a way to match-up the participation of players of different skill levels in competition events against teams of similar ability level (see Siedentop, Hastie, & Van der Mars, 2019).

Role-playing

In addition to the role of players, PE and sport contexts of less formally organized practice are very favourable settings for learners to perform other (complementary) roles of sport (e.g., refereeing, managing sporting events, records taking on performance and social interactions). Role-playing is a foundational pedagogy of some well-established pedagogical models such as Sport Education (Siedentop et al., 2019) and Cooperative Learning (Dyson & Casey, 2016). The literature has shown that youngsters' engagement in different role-playing assigns augmented authenticity to the learning experience as it helps learners to bridge the sporting experiences they are living in school or at the club with their ideas of the wider "cultural sport world".

Box 5.8 Key concept: role-playing, creativity, and sport culture

As argued in Chapter 8, the trajectory of students along their path of creativity can ultimately extend the cultural relevance of their experience through the applied connection of that experience to wider sport culture. Role-playing and the opportunity to actively participate in the management of sporting events that are significant to the school or club life has the potential to extend that experience to a meta-level. That is, a broader understanding of how learners' sporting experience connects with their real lives, trying to explicitly establish bridges between the two contexts.

Importantly, role-playing redefines learners' idea of competence and what being competent means. Being a skilful referee or coach should be as important as being a skilful game-player. Sport educators can attach an educational focus to role-playing activities that are explicitly aimed at promoting social consciousness and empathy attitudes. Below we present some role-playing activities:

The inclusion captain

The introduction and high importance assigned to the "inclusion captain" role can be a supplementary strategy for the active promotion of more democratic learning contexts. Learners rotate in the daily monitoring of discriminatory occurrences and levels of equity taking place in their teams and in the other teams. They should take records (team charts) on the level of inclusive and equitable behaviours and should report this information to the sport educator or to the "sports panel".

The analyst

The analyst is responsible for analysing game problems and the respective learning needs of their teams (see Chapter 12; peer- and self-assessment). In addition to the increased motivation for participating in practice (as a result of a deeper understanding of the game), learners also develop a deeper awareness of the weaknesses/strengths of their peers and increased self-knowledge of their personal capabilities and needs-improvement skills. These experiences empower the learner to participate more actively in sharing knowledge and giving feedback to their peers. Learners also develop a better sense of who to go to for help with their specific game-play problems. To succeed in these interactions, learners often need to bond with teammates with whom they had no previous affective ties.

The referee

While refereeing, learners in the role of players who are very critical of referees are likely to experience the complexity of analysing and making decisions in difficult and fast-shifting circumstances. This will compel learners to deal with the fact that they too make mistakes and how their attitudes impact the quality of social interactions with their peers.

The events sport manager

Self-centred individualistic learners showing low commitment in collaborative interactions are engaged in the organization of sporting events (e.g., tournaments) and high responsibility decision-making. This experience helps learners to value novel facets of their sporting experience.

The peer-coach

During presentation of peer-teaching tasks or when trying to lead teammates to buy-in into their ideas of team strategy, learners who often resist authority, are critical of their sport educators' decisions, or have an authoritarian attitude towards their peers are confronted with the need to communicate their ideas and intentions efficiently and empathically. Learners will realize that the nature of the interactions they establish with their peers strongly influences the success of their role-playing tasks. Learners will need to put considerable effort in being friendly and bonding with their teammates.

Sporting events

Both in youth sport practice and PE contexts, sporting events (competitions) can be created to provide opportunities for learning the cultural traditions of their institution and strengthen social bonds with other members of that community. Sport educators may create opportunities for learners to participate in game-play events with other members of the institution and players of different age groups. Namely:

- Participation as players in tournaments, competitions, and other sport events inside or outside the sport institution.
- Participation in the organization and management of sporting events in complementary roles: refereeing, sport manager, score keeping, coaching younger peers.
- Participation in mixed-ability competition games (players can play side by side with peers above/below their age and skill level to promote novel social interactions).
- Elder learners can play co-coaching roles while assisting the head coaches of younger aged learners.

Box 5.9 Key point: benefits of structural-based scaffolding

- Playing against peers of similar skill level promotes high level of engagement rates and playing efficiency of both lower- and higher-skilled learners.
- Learners of different genders and ability level can offer a valid contribution to their learning teams' achievement of game-play goals (e.g., records of team scores).
- Learners' perceptions of the benefits of collaborative and inclusive efforts will reinforce the commitment of dominant learners to nurture more inclusive game-play goals.

Contextual-based scaffolding

In a learner-oriented approach, sport educators seek to create a learning context that legitimizes different forms of individual participation and levels of motor competence. That is, a nurturing environment in which learners feel safe about who they are and about what they can contribute to the main goals (e.g., committed game-play participation) of their learning community (team).

The systematic embedding of **accountability strategies** in the teaching-learning process has the potential to generate a positive contextual climate in which learners are strongly energized to coalesce into a proactive search of socially empathetic, equitable, and inclusive interactions.

Box 5.10 Key concept: collective construction of winning and competence

A learner-oriented approach is grounded on the central need to scaffold a collaborative construction of collectively embodied meanings on an appreciation of "winning" and "competence" that legitimizes different levels of participation, contribution, and membership to a learning community.

In this regard we highlight **records and team chart** (embedding authenticity and meaning into learning activities) and the **awards and celebration** (public recognition of different levels of individual and collective accomplishment).

Records and team chart

Social development records[6]

The need for practitioners to exhibit an embodied appropriate ethical conduct during competitive or other practice events can be reinforced through formal accountability for these behaviours. If sport educators score in equal proportion game-play performance goals (skills-based task goals or scoring for victory) and learners' display of inclusive and morally decent attitudes (points for fair-play behaviours), it nurtures a learning climate in which it is just as important to strive to win as to nurture positive social interactions with their peers. Learners can be held accountable for numerous positive social attitudes (it will depend on the values framework that the coach educator wishes to foster): camaraderie, fair-play, peer-teaching and feedback attitudes, commitment, responsibility, organizational or digital technology skills, respect for peers, or showing active ethical attitudes to preserve equity and inclusion for all.

Inclusive performance records[7]

From an inclusion perspective, the trick is in what the coach educator chooses to highlight as an indicator of motor competence. The records may focus on the frequency of actions of specific collective motor responses (ball possessions and retrievals, number of attempted shots, scored shots, etc.) that do not necessarily allocate a direct and individualized qualitative assessment to the observed motor responses. Focusing on efficiency criteria also provides an opportunity to focus on process rather than on the immediate outcome of game actions.

Role-playing records

These records formalize the responsibility of practitioners in performing roles complementary to the role of players. It conveys the notion that learning and ability to perform these roles is also a "subject-matter" of sport.

Team chart

The team charts provide a visual and authentic tangible way for learners in persistent learning teams to map the ongoing outcomes of their work. The score chart cumulatively sums the various entry scores of the daily records taken by learners related to social, performance, and role-playing scores (see Chapter 11 for further details on how to use this strategy).

Awards and celebration

Certificate diplomas are **awards** that hold significant symbolic value to learners. They celebrate learners' full membership in a community of learning. Therefore, sport educators should promote regular events (at the end of the school term or between club competition stages) to publicly celebrate the multidimensional achievements of their sport learners. These events can be extended to the educational community in schools or to the families of the learners, in the case of sports clubs. These celebrations not only reinforce social bonding between learners, but also provide a reference against which children and young people can judge the relevance, authenticity, and outcome of the work they are carrying out.

The sport development process and the kind of learners' attitudes and dispositions that the sport educator chooses to recognize, emphasize, and value, send a clear message to the learners about the goals and attitudes to which they should aspire. We advise sport educators to celebrate merit related not only with learners' motor performance (e.g., best player/scorer/batter, best defender/attacker, best goalkeeper, etc.) but also relative to learners' self-referenced goals (e.g., learner who made the most progress in class) and development of personal and social skills (e.g., the best fair-play team, the most responsible learner, the fairest referee, etc.).

Box 5.11 Key point: benefits of contextual-based scaffolding

- Learners develop deep knowledge of their partners' personal attributes, potential weaknesses and strengths, they bond, and share knowledge and mutually motivating prompts.
- The lower-skilled learners develop skills and confidence leading to enhanced participation in game-play and consequent well-being and enjoyment.
- It creates a mastery-involving climate (e.g., no pressure on the girls to "be like the boys").

- Building a holistic process-oriented idea of sport development and competence creates a safe learning climate that provides mental freedom to learners to access and understand their needs-improvement issues (why did I miss the shot?) and to review and correct it (how can I improve it?).

Scaffolding learner-mediated social interactions

As in the instructional process (see Chapter 4), also in the social interaction dynamics that underpin the quality of such instructional interactions, the role of students themselves in leadership and responsibility roles can be a strong active mediator of the positive, democratic, and equitable learning dynamics emerging among children. Sport educators can implement numerous strategies to prepare peer-coaches, or the "inclusion captains", to mediate the emergence of positive social relationships between learners.

During pre- or post-session briefings and through video analysis of critical incidents in the sessions, the coach educator can encourage students in "social mediation" tasks to develop awareness and reflection that will help them identify potential intervention points.

The scaffolding of the peer-mediators' intervention can focus on:

- Identifying and acting on discriminatory, bullying, or inequitable social interactions ("how equitable were the on-the-ball participation opportunities granted to girls in the 3v2 task?").
- Be sensitive to provide positive feedback or publicly highlight the value and effort of less popular or less able learners to achieve their teams' collective goals (sport educator: "how can you acknowledge Rick's effort?"; peer-mediator: "perhaps, good job Rick, your determination made it difficult for them to score").
- Identify possible tensions or poor social bonding between particular students and establish a bridge between the mutual interests of these learners (e.g., "Jane is struggling with the overhead pass, who might be suitable to help her here?").
- Guide peer-mediators to pair students who are less socially bonded to each other in activities in which both can collaboratively contribute to task goals.
- Teach peer-mediators how to make their fellow learners accountable for their own equitable and democratic actions ("perhaps it would be interesting to find a way to make your teammates more

actively responsible for their conduct. How about, at the end of each task, ask them how many times they encouraged their mates or passed the ball around?").

Box 5.12 Key point: benefits of actively engaging learners in the mediation of positive social interactions

• Learners take on a more proactive regulation of the quality of their social interactions.
• Learners coalesce into the construction of collective meanings of equity and responsibility.
• Learners develop a heightened awareness of the importance of actively nurturing positive social interactions to contribute to the well-being of all and to a more just and equitable world.

Self-processing questions

Box 5.13 A time to reflect – content review

• Think back to your last few weeks of teaching or coaching practice and reflect on the extent to which you are promoting a democratic and wide-reaching meaningful participation of learners in sport and games.
• On that basis, write up what are you going to do in your next practice (introduce new scaffolding strategies, reinforce the use of current scaffolding strategies, etc.).
• What are the main components of structural- and contextual-based scaffolding of positive social interactions and learners' meaningful participation in sporting activities?

Summary and key points

Engaging learners in productive collaborative problem-solving interactions (whether they are game-play or social justice problems) requires the active implementation of scaffolding strategies by sport educators. The integration of sport panels and group reflection on social issues into the pacing of learning activities prompts learners to collectively construct meanings about positive ways of being and belonging to the sport community they are included in. Sport educators can also use their knowledge about task modifications and competition organization (graded competition) to promote more balanced and equitable participation of learners in the activities. To this purpose, several contextual scaffolding strategies may be applied to create a positive learning environment (role-playing, taking records). Finally, learners themselves can be "mandated" and empowered as active mediators of their teammates' meaningful participation in the instructional and social activities of their teams.

Notes

1 Especially in PE classes, or in youth sports coaching environments where the sport educator has the possibility to organize the whole team for participating in learning activities while affiliated into sub-learning teams that persist over time.
2 A comprehensive set of game modification strategies is provided in Chapter 7.
3 In southern Europe schools, it is very common in the PE football units to have a large gap in the ability level between students without extra-school experience and students with a background of systematic practice of the sport in clubs.
4 The sub-teams can practice the game against each other but applying different constraining or facilitating modifications for each sub-team. For example, in the lower-ability team, interception in the team's defensive zone can be prohibited, whereas the stronger team must play with defensive pressure from the beginning of setting up the attack starting from their goal zone.
5 Originally developed in the Sport Education model (Siedentop, Hastie, & Van der Mars, 2019) literature given its strong component of peer-teaching and "formal" competition activities.
6 Chapter 11 offers specific criteria and modes for assessing these social skills.
7 See Chapter 11 for specific performance-based assessment criteria and quantitative and narrative ways to ascertain inclusive, equity, and democratic attitudes in game-play activities.

References

Beni, S., Fletcher, T., & Ní Chróinín, D. (2017). Meaningful experiences in physical education and youth sport: A review of the literature. *Quest, 69*(3), 291–312.

Dyson, B., & Casey, A. (2016). *Cooperative learning in physical education and physical activity: A practical introduction*. London: Routledge.

Siedentop, D., Hastie, P., & Van der Mars, H. (2019). *Complete guide to sport education (3rd edition)*. Champaign, IL: Human Kinetics.

Part III

Designing Meaningful and Creative Learning Activities in Sport and Games

6 Appropriateness-Based Activities

Reaching Out to Every Learner

Ana Ramos, José Afonso, Patrícia Coutinho, Cristiana Bessa, Cláudio Farias and Isabel Mesquita

---

Box 6.1 Objectives

At the end of this chapter, you will be able to:

- Understand the appropriateness concept.
- Conjugate learners, goals, and tasks in a coherent learning framework, respecting intra- and inter-individual learning variation.
- Set educational goals according to the learners' characteristics and needs at each moment.
- Manipulate and adapt tasks to better accomplish the learner requirements.

Box 6.2 Key sections

- Introduction.
- Conceptual and practical principles of pedagogical appropriateness.
- Practical examples.

Introduction

To successfully implement a learner-oriented approach, sport educators must consider not only learners' individual characteristics (e.g., skill level) but also meet the instructional alignment between learning goals and the design of appropriate learning tasks[1] (Woods et al.,

DOI: 10.4324/9781003140016-9

2020). Besides the importance in leading the instructional process, the scaffolding process acquires a new dimension focused not only on designing, but also on monitoring and adapting the learning task. In this chapter, we argue that the educational goals can be reached through the concept of *appropriateness*: a pedagogical perspective to help educators structure and create meaningful learning environments (i.e., those that hold personal significance to learners; Beni, Fletcher, & Ní-Chrónín, 2017) for all learners, while respecting inter- and intra-individual variations in learning over time.

Although heavily influenced by interpersonal and interdependent domains (see Chapter 1), meaningful sport experiences are intrinsically personal, relying on the interplay among the learners' skills and their own learning goals (Chen, 1998), thus being deeply linked with the learners' "life history". By considering physical and/or skill-related goals, as well as establishing a close interplay between cognitive, psychological, and emotional domains (Curran & Standage, 2017), *appropriateness* emerges as a concept whose application varies depending on the individuals and the context in which they operate and build their sporting identity. In practical terms, appropriateness-based activities consider: (i) the unique motivations, experiences, and knowledge-background of each learner; and (ii) learning as a daily evolving process, with ongoing changes in learners' characteristics and needs. By attending to these premises, sport educators are more likely to design meaningful learning experiences (Storey & Butler, 2013).

In summary, this chapter maps the conceptual and practical implications of an appropriateness-based proposal for teaching and learning sport and games which emerges from the interaction between three domains of the teaching-learning process: the learners' characteristics (level I), the educational goals (level II), and the design of learning tasks (level III). We offer sport educators a progressive, scaffolded structure of practical examples on how to apply appropriateness-based principles in the design of sport activities for different game categories (e.g., invasion, non-invasion, fielding-striking games).

Conceptual and practical principles of pedagogical appropriateness

The principles supporting the appropriateness-based activities align with constructivist approaches to learners learning (Zhang, Wang, Yli-Piipari, & Chen, 2021). The learners are at the centre of the teaching-learning process and play an active role in developing knowledge (Mesquita et al., 2015). An appropriateness-based proposal relies on four interacting premises.

Premise 1: The learners should be at the
core of educational processes

To place the learners at the core of the learning process implies that pre-established goals, especially if fixed and uniform, will likely fail to address the different learning needs of different learners. If all learners are expected to achieve the same goals within similar timelines (one-size-fits-all approach), they will stop being individuals in their own right, becoming instruments of an external "dissemination" of pre-determined goals.

Learners are expected to play an active role in creating higher degrees of appropriateness, in a gradual and scaffolded process (see Chapter 4). This is in sharp contrast with the reality of most school systems, where Physical Education (PE) classes have a fixed or semi-fixed baseline of activities and learning goals (with largely fixed assessment benchmarks) for each class and/or stage of learning. We advocate a flexible approach to the education of youngsters through participation in sport and games, with freedom for each school to adjust the goals and contents to their own context, and with the benchmarks being open to discussion and change at any moment.

Hence, the process of "reaching out" to every learner by designing appropriate learning environments implies the recognition and development of the intra- and inter-individual variability of sport learners (Kliegel & Altgassen, 2006). The intra-individual variability refers to the variation in learning of an individual at different moments, while inter-individual variability refers to the variations among different learners. In practical terms, variability could be addressed through the inclusion of variants (e.g., different levels of complexity) in learning tasks, or by setting different learning goals, as we show in the next premise (see also Box 6.5, examples 1 and 2). The design of appropriateness-based tasks is only achieved when the state of learning readiness of each learner is considered. Therefore, sport educators must be aware of the differences in the learning pacing of every learner.

Premise 2: Learning goal-setting must be highly individualized

Connected with high pedagogical individualisation, goal-setting must follow a dynamic and socially informed venture. As learners and contexts evolve differentially, the learning goals must be continuously re-assessed and re-drawn to ensure the *appropriateness* of these proposals to the learners' needs. Thus, sport educators embrace the non-linearity of learning (Afonso, Clemente, Ribeiro, Ferreira, &

Fernandes, 2020; Rivera-Pérez, Fernandez-Rio, & Gallego, 2021), namely:

i   While some learning goals may inevitably align with learners' growth and development within societal requirements, most educational goals should be individualized.
ii Proper diagnosis of who learners are as individuals and what drives them to participate in sport-based activities (i.e., their motivations, aspirations, skills, personality) play a nuclear role in the evolving setting of PE or youth coach goals.

In this vein, flexibility and adaptability are of the utmost importance; hence, goals should not be set in stone. During the implementation of learning tasks, sport educators should be attentive to how well the learners understood the task goal and dynamics (i.e., its structure) and whether the task is useful to reach the goals set. Thereby, the scaffolding process acquires a new dimension focused not only on the design of the task, but also on its ongoing monitoring. The task should be adapted (when necessary) so that the goals of learning and tasks are closely aligned with current learners' ability and needs (see Box 6.5, example 3). Accordingly, it is crucial to know what is fundamental to each learner, or small group of learners, at each moment to effectively design the most appropriate learning environments.

Premise 3: Representativeness must be extended

Appropriateness requires an extension of the representativeness concept, not only limited to how well a task will translate into performance outcomes (i.e., be more effective at playing some sport), but also strongly focused on the learners' features and motivations. The goal is also to contribute to wider social and cultural development. In a learner-oriented approach, the term "representative" refers to the learning of game-based content, and to the individual's learning process. Thus, appropriateness-based activities seek an active and evolving commitment of learners with their learning process, and an embodied ability to cope with the multiple challenges within the process of learning sport and becoming successful players and citizens (Farias, Wallhead, & Mesquita, 2020).

Appropriateness emerges when learners are personally engaged in the active development of their own, and their peers' learning process, with concerns that far surpass those exclusive of sports performance. To this purpose, the learning experience becomes representative when sport educators create contexts that value the unique and innate capabilities of different learners (e.g., through accountability strategies) or generate positive social interactions among learners that will enable their access to a fuller participation in the learning experience (see Chapter 5, and Box 6.6). Specifically, accountability is considered as a critical component of the teaching-learning process (Griffin, Mitchell, & Oslin, 1997) and refers to instructional processes used to transfer responsibility to learners so that they can be accountable for, and engaged with, their own learning (Pereira, Mesquita, & Graça, 2009). In an appropriateness-based proposal, informal (e.g., monitoring learners' performance, defining task criteria) and formal (e.g., learning assessment through competitive situations) accountability systems should be used.

Premise 4: Learning goals must be translated into meaningful tasks

A solid understanding of the learners' characteristics, together with the flexible and evolving design of well-adjusted goals and benchmarks, is merely the first step sport educators should undertake. To translate learning goals into meaningful tasks in an appropriateness framework implies the nurturing of equity [i.e., to give, to celebrate, and to consider the social and cultural differences of individuals during educational settings (Penney, 2002); see Chapter 5].

The translation of goals into tasks requires identifying the critical components (e.g., within an invasion game context, to create or close space with or without ball possession, respectively), and interpreting how such components could be implemented to reach the intended goal. Quite often, pragmatic considerations about contextual, material, and human resources become highly relevant. To exemplify, the number of learners, ratio of sport educators per learners, usable sport facilities, available material, safety considerations, among other details must be considered to provide a meaningful and effective learning experience. Sport educators may anticipate issues inherent to the teaching-learning process, but there are unforeseen problems that emerge in real-life contexts.

Grounded on the abovementioned, appropriateness-based activities include three levels of appropriateness (Figure 6.1):

- **Level 1**: identify the learners' characteristics and needs and establish goals that are aligned with both. Respect for inter-individual and intra-individual variation is expected.
- **Level 2**: design tasks aligned with the goals, as well as the available conditions for implementing them. These tasks should be

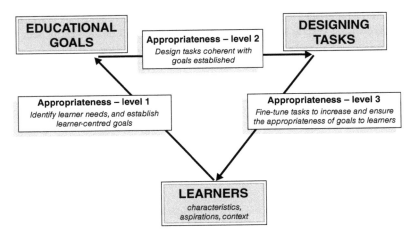

Figure 6.1 Building appropriateness-based activities in a learner-oriented approach.

representative to express the formal performance settings, but also wider individual and societal educational expectations that are required of school and youth sport institutions.

– **Level 3**: observe how the task is unfolding and, if necessary, adjust it to improve the original task design and strengthen the appropriateness for learners who are performing it.

Practical tasks

Appropriateness level -1: understanding who and where the learners are and setting goals

---

Box 6.3 Task: diagnosis of learners' needs

LEARNING CONTENTS: Technical and tactical actions of a basketball game.

PURPOSE: (i) To diagnose the learners' skill in two different game scenarios: with ball possession – creating space and passing lines, score; without ball possession – closing space and blocking opponents' passing lines, protect the basket; (ii) to set learning goals for the next pedagogical intervention.

EXAMPLE: Small-sided basketball game: 3v3.

At the first level of the appropriateness-based proposal it is necessary to diagnose the learners features and needs to set coherent learning goals (Box 6.3). Thus, the learner is placed at the core of the educational process. The sport educator diagnoses the learners' game-play ability, while observing whether their motivations align with the expectations of the sport educator. For instance, by using small-sided games (e.g., 3v3), the sport educator can grasp the level of learners' game skills and how they understand the game. From this opening point, the sport educator establishes task goals that best suit that class or group of learners. Through a progressively scaffolded process, it is expected that learners engage in a progressively more active role in setting the goals and task design, as aspects discussed, for example in Chapters 4 and 8.

Next, acknowledging and respecting the inter-individual and intra-individual variation among learners, the sport educator might realize that learners are heterogeneous at several levels. Perhaps some learners need to improve their technical skills to be able to play the game, while others may have proficient technique, but do not make the best decisions during the game. Another group may demotivate excessively when facing poor results. Yet other learners may lack the endurance to keep their performance during the game. The take-home message is that most likely there will be complex combinations between several dimensions of learning.

Based on the diagnosis, the sport educator establishes three levels of learning goals (and preferably discusses and builds these goals with an increasingly active participation of learners):

i Class-level goals, to address learning problems and opportunities that may be relevant for the entire group.
ii Group-level goals, to consider the difficulties and opportunities for different groups of learners.
iii Individual-level goals, to provide an extra challenge for the few higher-skilled learners, or to provide less-skilled learners with better tools to cope with the task demands when integrated with more skilled learners.

Box 6.4 Key concept: ongoing adjustment of learning goals

The learning goals established at the outset will guide the instructional process, but they should be adjusted over time (Premise 2). Sport educators should consider whether learners show quicker, slower, or simply different adaptations. Two procedures are possible:

- The goals are valid, but novel implementations should be designed.
- The goals need to be adapted.

These procedures should be shared with learners so that they can engage actively in building their own learning processes.

To illustrate with an arbitrary example of what could be a real-life case: sport educators assess learners' responses and decide that they lack dribbling skills, which is impairing their offensive play ability. Moreover, learners seem to be very individualistic and unsupportive when their teammates make a mistake. Two core developmental goals are set: to improve dribbling skills, but also to promote a greater sense of teamwork and team identity.[2]

Appropriateness level -2: translating educational goals into concrete learning tasks

Based on the pre-established goals, the sport educator decides to adapt the dribbling tasks (in Chapters 4 and 8 we show how learners may play an active role in designing learning tasks). Accordingly, the examples next presented are similar in their content development (i.e., ball control; class-level goal), but adapted with different levels of difficulty (i.e., facing different types of opposition; group-level goals) based on learners' skill level. Also, by adapting the space between defenders, the sport educator is individualizing learning goals (i.e., individual-level goals). Such adaptations enable the sport educator to plan and work according to each learners' needs, making the learning environment appropriate for reaching out to every learner. In addition, by using a score system to award an appropriate action (informal accountability system), educators can focus the learners' attention on one of the most tactical components of playing basketball: removing the eyes from the ball. The inclusion of static opposition affords representativity to the learning task once the learners are confronted with opposition (in a simplified fashion) featured from competition.

Box 6.5 Task: adjusting constraints to suit learners of different skills

LEARNING CONTENTS: Dribbling against static and dynamic defenders.

PURPOSE: (i) Ball control; (ii) increasing the sense of teamwork.

CRITICAL COMPONENTS: Removing the eyes from the ball.

EXAMPLE 1: In the lower-skilled group, each learner has their own ball and will dribble it through a circuit where passive defenders play the role of a static opponent; the last element of the group is on the opposite side of the circuit, providing feedback so that the dribbler look at them. Each time the dribbler can regularly look to the teammate, the group scores a point. The teammates not involved in dribbling are coaching the dribbler, providing technical feedback.

EXAMPLE 2: The high-level group performs the same task, but the defenders provide slight active opposition: if the dribbler successfully passes through them, there is no further pursuit. The space between defenders is adapted according to the abilities of each learner.

EXAMPLE 3: Lower-skilled learners who were performing the task successfully are challenged to perform the task against defenders who cannot intercept the ball (arms braced behind backs) but can use footwork to disturb the dribbling action.

Appropriateness level -3: fine-tune tasks to increase and ensure the appropriateness of goals to learners

The task is now being performed by the learners, but another problem emerges: some learners from the higher-skilled group are too advanced to engage in the version that is being performed by the lower-skilled group. Given this scenario, the sport educator fine-tunes the task using a *regression*. This represents a clear example of reducing intra-task complexity and variability (Box 6.5, example 1). Given this scenario, the sport educator fine-tuned the task using a regression. The sport educator also notes that some learners in the lower-skilled group were performing the task too easily, but perhaps were not quite ready for the tasks being performed by the higher-skilled group. Therefore, a *progression* task is created (Box 6.5, example 3).

These processes can be enhanced and accelerated by the implementation of peer-coaching strategies, whereby the learners actively try to teach their peers (see Chapter 4). This feature will be important for the commitment of learners in their learning activities. The sport educator may establish task accountability criteria that acknowledges different levels of goal achievement for different learners while attributing similar importance to such achievements.[3] The example presented in Box 6.6 tries to accomplish this intention in a competitive context.

Box 6.6 Task 3: designing competitive game scenarios

LEARNING CONTENTS: Dribbling within competitive scenarios (3v3 game).

PURPOSE: Ball control; increasing the sense of team identity.

CRITICAL COMPONENTS: Dribbling before passing; higher-skilled learners cannot use their arms when defending lower-skilled learners.

EXAMPLE: The teams include learners from both skill levels. The sports educator implements a 3v3 game, in which a minimum of 5 dribbling actions must be performed before passing the ball to a teammate. The higher-skilled learners are instructed to act as peer-coaches, helping the lower-skilled learners through specific feedback and motivational prompts.

The dribbling action highlighted (i.e., 5 dribbling before pass) provides learners a contrast between the performance of this skill in structured and competitive tasks. Moreover, practicing the dribble action within learning scenarios representative of the competition provides a meaning to that action (extending representativeness concept and translating goals to meaningful tasks; premise 3 and 4, respectively).

Appropriateness implies individualized goals, but also considers that individuals are part of a higher social and cultural dimension (e.g., the class, the team). On some occasions, the sport educator chooses to form homogeneous groups, where each group works according to its specific needs and skills. On other occasions, the option is the formation of heterogeneous groups, to accelerate the evolution of the lower-skilled learners, but also promote mentoring by the higher-skilled learners (e.g., peer-coaching), while at the same time increasing true, class-level teamwork.

Self-processing questions

Box 6.7 A time to reflect – content review

- What are the premises of the appropriateness-based framework?
- At what levels should appropriateness-based activities be established?
- What is the difference between progression and regression principles? When should we apply each principle?
- Why should the concept of representativeness be expanded? How can we do it in practice?

Summary and key points

This chapter addressed the conceptual and practical applications of an appropriateness-based proposal for teaching and learning sport activities, including an extension of the concept of representativeness to reconcile performance-related features with individual and societal-related demands. In this sense, the pedagogical content of appropriateness is highly relevant to sport-based learning not only as a conceptual guide, but also as a practical method, especially because: (i) it presents a learner-oriented perspective; (ii) it sets individualized learning goals that are constantly revisited and adjusted; and (iii) it promotes equity through the individualization of learning goals and tasks. As will be explored in Chapters 10 and 11, this may not be fully compatible with pre-established benchmarks and rigid assessment instruments.

This framework may help sport educators design appropriate learning tasks more easily. Specifically, level-1 refers to the identification of learners' characteristics and needs, followed by the definition of learning goals aligned with both. Level-2 comprises the designing of tasks that addresses the established goals considering the facilities available. Finally, at level-3 should be observed how the task is unfolding, and adjusting it, if necessary.

Acknowledging the nonlinear fashion of learning, this framework underlines the vital role of sport educators in scaffolding the intra- and inter-learning development. Sport educators must analyse whether goals and/or tasks are fitting the learners' requirements, what inherently implies an ongoing assessment and adjustment of learning environments.

Notes

1 See the definition of Zone of Proximal Development and Scaffolding in Chapters 3 and 4.
2 This can easily follow a progressive set of social scaffolding procedures such as those offered in Chapter 5; e.g., sport panels, reflective group discussions, taking records, and scoring learners' positive and inclusive social interactions.
3 See Structural-based and Contextual-based scaffolding in Chapter 5.

References

Afonso, J., Clemente, F. M., Ribeiro, J., Ferreira, M., & Fernandes, R. J. (2020). Towards a de facto nonlinear periodization: Extending nonlinearity from programming to periodizing. *Sports, 8*(8), 110. doi:10.3390/sports8080110

Beni, S., Fletcher, T., & Ní-Chrónín, D. (2017). Meaningful experiences in physical education and youth sport: A review of the literature. *Quest, 69*(3), 291–312. doi: 10.1080/00336297.2016.1224192

Chen, A. (1998). Meaningfulness in physical education: A description of high school students' conceptions. *Journal of Teaching in Physical Education, 17*(3), 285. doi: 10.1123/jtpe.17.3.285

Curran, T., & Standage, M. (2017). Psychological needs and the quality of student engagement in physical education: Teachers as key facilitators. *Journal of Teaching in Physical Education, 36*(3), 262–276. doi: 10.1123/jtpe.2017–0065

Farias, C., Wallhead, T., & Mesquita, I. (2020). "The project changed my life": Sport education's transformative potential on student physical literacy. *Research Quarterly for Exercise and Sport, 91*(2), 263–278. doi: 10.1080/02701367.2019.1661948

Gagné, M. (2018). From strategy to action: Transforming organizational goals into organizational behavior. *International Journal of Management Reviews, 20*(S1), 83–104. doi: 10.1111/ijmr.12159

Griffin, L., Mitchell, S., & Oslin, J. (1997). *Teaching sport concepts and skills: A tactical game approach.* Cahmpaign, IL: Human kinetics.

Kliegel, M., & Altgassen, M. (2006). Interindividual differences in learning performance: The effects of age, intelligence, and strategic task approach. *Educational Gerontology, 32*(2), 111–124. doi: 10.1080/03601270500388133

Mesquita, I., Coutinho, P., Martin-Silva, L. d., Parente, B., Faria, M., & Afonso, J. (2015). The value of indirect teaching strategies in enhancing student-coaches' learning engagement. *Journal of Science and Medicine, 14*, 657–668.

Penney, D. (2002). Equality, equity and inclusion in physical education and school sport. In A. Laker (Ed.), *The Sociology of Sport and Physical Education: An Introductory Reader* (1st ed., pp. 110–128). London: Routledge.

Pereira, F., Mesquita, I., & Graça, A. (2009). Accountability systems and instructional approaches in youth volleyball training. *Journal of Sports Science and Medicine, 8,* 366–373.

Rivera-Pérez, S., Fernandez-Rio, J., & Gallego, D. I. (2021). Effects of an 8-week cooperative learning intervention on physical education students' task and self-approach goals, and emotional intelligence. *International Journal of Environmental Research and Public Health, 18*(1), 61. doi: 10.3390/ijerph18010061

Storey, B., & Butler, J. (2013). Complexity thinking in PE: Game-centred approaches, games as complex adaptive systems, and ecological values. *Physical Education & Sport Pedagogy, 18*(2), 133–149. doi: 10.1080/17408989.2011.649721

Woods, C. T., McKeown, I., Rothwell, M., Araújo, D., Robertson, S., & Davids, K. (2020). Sport practitioners as sport ecology designers: How ecological dynamics has progressively changed perceptions of skill "acquisition" in the sporting habitat. *Frontiers in Psychology, 11*(624), 1–15. doi: 10.3389/fpsyg.2020.00654

Zhang, T., Wang, Y., Yli-Piipari, S., & Chen, A. (2021). Power of the curriculum: Content, context, and learning in physical education. *Research Quarterly for Exercise and Sport, 92*(4), 689–700. doi: 10.1080/02701367.2020.1768202

Additional resources

Button, C., Seifert, L., Chow, J. Y., Araújo, D., & Davids, K. (2020). *Dynamics of skill acquisition: An ecological dynamics approach* (2nd ed.). Champaign, IL: Human Kinetics.

Fletcher, T., Chróinín, D. N., Gleddie, D., & Beni, S. (2021). *Meaningful physical education: An approach for teaching and learning* (T. Fletcher, D. N. Chróinín, D. Gleddie, & S. Beni Eds. 1st ed.). London: Routledge.

7 Constraints-Led Approach

Appropriately Modifying Learning Activities

Pedro Tiago Esteves and Bruno Travassos

Box 7.1 Objectives

At the end of this chapter, you will be able to:

- Adopt practical-based principles of a constraints-led approach to teaching and learning
- Apply evidence-based knowledge for the manipulation of individual, task, and environmental constraints across different sports categories
- Recognize and implement different possibilities for practice-task design

---

Box 7.2 Key sections

- Introduction
- Principles for the design of learning activities
- Effects of constraints manipulation
- Practical tasks

Introduction

With this chapter we aim to provide sport educators with a hands-on overview on how the Constraints-led Approach (CLA), underpinned by nonlinear pedagogy principles, can add value to the teaching-learning process. In addition, we seek to cover up-to-date scientific evidence on the potential effect of constraints manipulation across different sport games. Finally, practical examples will also be provided to illustrate how the theoretical grounding and scientific evidence can inform the design of learner-oriented activities.

DOI: 10.4324/9781003140016–10

In the late few years, the CLA has been advocated as a prominent framework for the development of skill acquisition across different sport domains. The CLA posits that learning and development take place at the level of the ecological scale of individual-environment interaction under the effect of evolving constraints (Davids, Button, & Bennett, 2008). Such process is overarched by nonlinear pedagogical principles that conceive human behaviour as inherently nonlinear in character. For instance, the behavioural fluctuations observed during each practice, and over the learning process, should be assumed as a process of learners' progressive ability to explore functional movement solutions within the available possibilities for action (Renshaw, Davids, Shuttleworth, & Chow, 2009). To promote such a discovery process, sport educators should ensure that the identification and manipulation of relevant constraints facilitate the self-organization (i.e., spontaneous emergence) of movement solutions (Renshaw et al., 2009). This empirical-based intervention is critical to achieve a desirable level of consistency along the teaching-learning process.

Constraints are conceived as boundaries that shape movement solutions over the course of action (Gray, 2020). In this way, they should not be misinterpreted as a limitation or negative influence on the development process of sport learners as they exert a direct influence on the assembly of specific movement patterns (Sullivan, Woods, Vaughan, & Davids, 2021). Typically, constraints can be divided in three categories: individual (person's characteristics), environment (surrounding context characteristics), and task (activity related characteristics) (Newell, 1986). An example of individual constraints could be the height, expertise, or the emotional state of the learner. Conversely, task constraints stand as the most common and immediate possibility for manipulation as it relates to the goals, rules or equipment implicated in the learning task. Environmental constraints are more challenging to manipulate, but playing in front of an audience, or with great wind intensity may stand as illustrative examples. Whilst this division may be prone to a given subjectivity, its systematization is of high relevance for sport educators' efficient designing of educational environments. These three categories of constraints continuously interact to influence and guide the process of learning and the emergence of certain possibilities for action. Thus, sport educators, through the selective manipulation of different constraints, could create appropriate learning contexts that guide each learner to discover unique movement solutions to the task at hand (Chow, Davids, Hristovski, Araújo, & Passos, 2011). Alongside, the provision of clear and applied principles for the design of learning activities is of foremost importance to achieve a desired level of coherence between theory and practice.

Principles for the design of learning activities

In this section four key principles underpinned by nonlinear pedagogy were described to improve the richness and engagement of learning environments (Renshaw et al., 2009).

Preserving the link between perception and action (i.e., perception-action coupling)

Learning activities should contain the representativeness principle at the highest possible extension. They should consider the tight coupling between information and actions. So, learning activities should be designed to integrate key information sources and actions together as they occur in the most representative performance environment (e.g., the formal version of the sport, if this is the case). In volleyball for instance, the contact of the hand on the ball during the overhand serve is closely bounded with previously tossing the ball up into the air. Designing a task that only allows for the athlete to strike the ball will decouple the perceptual and motor components.

Implementing task simplification

To facilitate goal achievement, instead of either removing important information from the practical context (e.g., scoring targets) or decoupling perception and action (e.g., remove the opponent in a basketball defensive shuffle), an alternative strategy should imply task simplification. Simplification involves a selective manipulation of constraints to limit the relevant information that supports task goals and facilitates goal achievements (see regression/progression in Chapter 6). For instance, in basketball, a defender must perform a defensive shuffle to maintain a desired alignment with the attacker in ball possession and prevent a successful shot. A task simplification in these exemplar task could be developed by constraining the actions of the attacker in ball possession to a given playing area, or to a given range of movement velocity to create more favourable conditions for the defender to maintain the alignment with the attacker and the basket.

Promoting variability in learning contexts

Variability is essential for the process of discovering new possibilities for action that sustain adaptability and flexibility in the learning process according to the individual's characteristics. Therefore, the design of learning environments should critically balance the range of possible movement solutions for the learner to explore and its own action capabilities to set up an adapted level of challenge and development. By "repeating without repeating", the sport learner is consistently exposed to a process of searching a functional task solution while mastering their own degrees of freedom (i.e., body components such as joints, muscles, bones, etc.) (Bernstein, 1967). For example, a pass in volleyball co-implicates, at least, two players and can be performed with a large range of variation in the game both from an individual or relational perspective. Accordingly, training tasks should accommodate this span of variability with the purpose of further developing adaptive movement patterns either by changing angles and distances between performers, size of ball, position in the pitch, etc.

Favouring feedback with an external focus

To ensure that the intervention of the sport educators enhances the exploration of individual possibilities for action, the provision of feedback with an external focus should be prioritized. By highlighting the functional consequences of actions, learners can be challenged to search for new individual movement solutions (Peh, Chow, & Davids, 2011). For instance, in football more than simply directing feedback to movement kinematics (e.g., "follow-through"), sport educators should emphasize the functional consequences of the action in straight connection with the conditions of the environment that sustain specific possibilities for action (e.g., "contact the ball in a way to increase the speed and directness of ball trajectory towards the receiver's position") by promoting individual adjustments to achieve the goal.

Effects of constraints manipulation

In the remainder of this chapter, we will present evidence-based manipulation of constraints across different sports (invasion, target, and striking-fielding games) in an attempt to elucidate how sport educators can harness learners' game-based development. A CLA to sport games has posited that sport educators should consider the manipulation of key task constraints such as playing space, number of players, task instructions when designing learning environments (Coito, Davids, Folgado, Bento, & Travassos, 2020; Sgrò, Bracco, Pignato, & Lipoma, 2018). By systemically linking empirical evidence and practical purpose, sport educators may take advantage of a selective manipulation of existing constraints to achieve specific behavioural purposes.

Manipulation of playing space

The manipulation of playing space is one of the most powerful options to foster players' development. Examples of this kind of manipulation include, the spatial orientation of the pitch (in width, depth), the inclusion of spatial references (e.g., court lanes, sectors) or the playing space per player. Instead of prescribing a given game playing pattern, such as moving the ball through the lateral lane, the sport educator can choose to manipulate the spatial features (i.e., designing a wider pitch) to favour the exploration of the most functional solution to the task at hand (i.e., players exploring the exceptional space in width to move the ball into the opponent's goal). In football, for example, reshaping the spatial orientation of the field, introducing spatial references, or changing the number of goals stand as feasible solutions to promote specific game-play adaptations (e.g., variability of distances between players and teams) (Coito et al., 2020). Likewise, the use of different spatial orientations of the field (i.e., goals in the width, length or in diagonal defining a diamond) may also influence the effort and the level of synchronization between players by promoting distinct exploration and space occupations of the field (e.g., irregular fields promoted lower effort and higher variability in field occupation revealing an increase in exploratory individual behaviours). The manipulation of spatial references (i.e., sectors, lanes, squares for play) should be applied to enhance individual adaptations within the dynamics of the team. From a practical perspective, this option may favour the creation of specific 1v1, 2v1 (or other numerical relations), within a playing area, to explore numerical superiority within the team dynamics. Exemplarily, by increasing of the number of goals the opportunities to succeed in shooting at the goal are concomitantly increased. This option could be especially fruitful at early stages of player development.

Box 7.3 Key concept: exploring a practical purpose of pitch manipulation

Did you know that Chelsea Manager, Thomas Tuchel, has stated in public that he makes use of a diamond-shaped football pitch to encourage the execution of diagonal moves?

https://www.theguardian.com/football/2016/apr/07/thomas-tuchel-borussia-dortmund-jurgen-klopp.

Sport educators may also reduce the time and space available for action by shortening the playing space. As the distances between teammates and opponents get shorter, the variability of teams' behaviour tends to increase while ball possession time decreases, particularly in youth players. The reduction in the playing space is also related with an increase in the frequency of dribbling, tackles, and shots on goal (Sgrò et al., 2018). However, the available space needs to be adjusted to the individual capabilities of learners, since a small space of play requires higher perceptual capability, coordination, and speed of execution. Thus, in youth players with lower expertise, sport educators should use larger spaces of play that may allow adequate space and time for players to perceive and act within the game context. Worth noting is that the manipulation of playing space may also generate important physiological impacts. For instance, smaller pitches tend also to induce higher demands in terms of movement variability, changes of direction, and agility (Sarmento et al., 2018). Similar results were also obtained in tennis in which the reduction of court size and the net height, according to a scaling ratio, allowed young tennis performers to achieve a higher level of efficacy (e.g., greater winners ratio) along with a greater exploration of the areas near the net (e.g., a smaller number of balls stroked from behind the baseline) (Timmerman et al., 2015).

Also in net games, the manipulation of specific areas as targets has showed to potentially influence players' behaviours. In volleyball, there is evidence suggesting that the delimitation of two target areas (i.e., zone 1 v zone 5) appears to constrain the type of pass utilized by the players for ball reception. While the overhand pass was more frequent in zone 5, the zone 1 was more associated to the underhand pass. These results indicate that the players were able to flexibly adapt their movement behaviours to the evolving constraints while keeping up with a high level of performance (Paulo, Zaal, Fonseca, & Araújo, 2016). From a practical perspective, sport practitioners could take advantage of a selective manipulation of these task-related constraints to enhance movement solutions of their learners. Examples of such are manipulating the height of the net to facilitate or to limit a certain type of serve or changing receiver's initial position to promote specific player combinations.

Manipulation of the number of players

The variation in the *number of players* may notably impact, at first instance, the amount of information that players must attend (Sarmento et al., 2018). Let's take as an example a 2v2 or a 7v7 in handball. For a defender, the number of informational sources to perceive in a 2v2 include the direct opponent and an additional attacker. Contrarily, in the 7v7 there are six more attackers to monitor beyond the direct opponent. The amount of information can also be viewed with respect to the coordination between players of the same team. By attending to the previous example, the spatial and temporal coordination between seven defenders to close the gaps near the goal is much more demanding than in the 2v2 situation. The fact that players at the early stages of development show a low level of interpersonal coordination should account as has an important facet to properly design training tasks aimed at the enhancement of spatial-temporal relationships with teammates and opponents (Coito et al., 2020).

As the number of players in the task is increased, the interpersonal distance rises while the number of individual actions performed decreases and the available space and time for decisions and actions to take place is also impacted (Sarmento et al., 2018). From an individual level, a greater number of players also involves fewer actions with the ball and scoring attempts, although with less positional variability. Therefore, we suggest that the process of learning should entail a reduced number of players, especially at early stages of learning, to favour the *attunement* to relevant informational sources (i.e., consistent utilization of information) from teammates and opponents. This option may also benefit the intensification of individual actions while contributing to an enhanced level of adaptability and creativity. From a physiological perspective, the reduction in the number of players may increase the physical demands. Therefore, this potential manipulation should comply with the effective ability for the players to sustain task demands (Sarmento et al., 2018).

Box 7.4 Key concept: exploring a practical purpose on the manipulation of the number of players

Did you know that Horst Wein, a former youth hockey and soccer coach, supported the process of youth development based on the manipulation of the number of players in different game exercises?

https://www.amazon.com/Developing-Youth-Football-Players-Horst/dp/0736069488.

In general, the creation of numerical unbalance in invasion sports, such as a 2v1, shows the potential to highlight a range of action possibilities without a prior prescription of specific behaviours by the sport educators. In case of a task with numerical superiority, the possibility to pass to the teammate, to progress with the ball, or to hit the ball to the free space stand as prominent paths to achieve task goals, within a close relation with game circumstances. In invasion sports, to exploit numerical advantage, the ball carrier needs to control the ball and attract the opponent (i.e., decreasing their interpersonal distance over time, and creating a passing line to the teammate). Along the task, the possibility to pass or to further progress with the ball is perceived based on the variation of the defender position according to ball carrier displacement and the position of the ball receiver. Thus, we recommend the use of numerical superiority in the attack team to enhance the creation of passing lines for progression or shooting, and the use of numerical inferiority in the defence to improve space occupation and the level of coordination between defenders.

Manipulation of equipment

In net-wall games there are some interesting studies mostly focused on the positive influence of scaling equipment (racquet size, ball compression, court-size, net height, etc.) on movement behaviours of sport learners. One of such studies (Buszard, Farrow, Reid, & Masters, 2014) demonstrated that hitting performance of young performers was enhanced by the use of a smaller racquet combined with tennis balls with less compression. Potential effects of this scaling equipment were also reported in terms of the refinement of movement coordination patterns (swinging from low to high and striking the ball in front and to the side of the body). Of note is the fact that children appeared to be more sensitive to the possibilities for action that a given racquet size may disclose as the medium size was preferred over the smallest one.

Equipment scaling has been associated to an improved performance in youth sport learners across different sports. Notably, there is recent evidence showing in striking-fielding games that further modifications to regular-scaled equipment can improve skill acquisition and batting performance. The use of a larger surface area of cricket equipment (bats and balls) was associated with an enhanced batting pattern as well as higher batting performance, when compared to regular-sized equipment (Dancy & Murphy, 2020). Importantly, the promotion of variability in movement execution, for instance by using a modified hockey ball, can also seem to contribute to fostering skill acquisition in young learners (Brocken, van der kapm, Lenoir, & Savelsbergh, 2020). Taken together, this evidence provides additional support for sport educators to properly modify the equipment to facilitate skill acquisition across different sports especially by targeting youth sport population.

Box 7.5   Key concept: appropriately sized equipment facilitates learning

Did you know that skill acquisition could be hindered, and potentially regress, when using inappropriately sized equipment? https://www.nature.com/articles/s41598-020-59475-5.

Manipulation of task instructions

In net-wall games the manipulation of task instruction has also been explored as a means to uncover potential effects on passing actions (Barsingerhorn, Zaal, De Poel, & Pepping, 2013). Let's take as an example a 1v1 ball reception and passing task where three conditions were prescribed to the participants: free selection of passing action, overhead or underhand pass. When the participants were allowed to freely select the technical actions, the landing zone of the ball constrained the action chosen. For instance, for greater player-ball distances the underhand solution was more prevalent. Interestingly, the decision-making process in volleyball seems to be highly dependent on the possibilities for action arising from the manipulation of task instruction as well as spatial-temporal information associated with ball trajectory. These findings provide support for sport educators to focus more on the development of player sensitivity to action boundaries according to the available possibilities for action, instead of prescribing a "correct" movement solution.

Practical tasks

In this section we will provide several exemplary tasks that intend to illustrate how the implementation of a CLA to the sport game of futsal can facilitate learners' development. Based on the main goal of developing passing actions, a sequence of three tasks was designed to promote the exploration and discovering of the possibilities to pass (either with left or right foot) according to the manipulation of specific task constraints (space of play, spatial referents, number of players, rules of the task). Along these tasks, sport performers are progressively invited to be attuned to the information that supports changes in the body orientation of the ball carrier before ball reception to effectively support passing. Concurrently, the feedback should highlight the fit between the participants and the environment of play.

In the first task, the use of cones highlights different passing receptions and directions by assisting the sport performers to discover passes with left and right foot (Figure 7.1, upper panel). While the opponents were removed as a means to further simplify the task, performers are obliged to always see all the participants to monitor

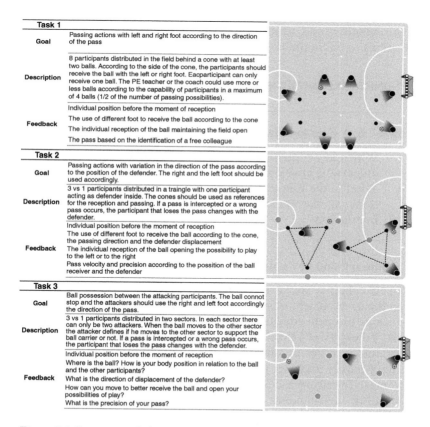

Task 1	
Goal	Passing actions with left and right foot according to the direction of the pass
Description	8 participants distributed in the field behind a cone with at least two balls. According to the side of the cone, the participants should receive the ball with the left or right foot. Eacparticipant can only receive one ball. The PE teacher or the coach could use more or less balls according to the capability of participants in a maximum of 4 balls (1/2 of the number of passing possibilities).
Feedback	Individual position before the moment of reception
	The use of different foot to receive the ball according to the cone
	The individual reception of the ball maintaining the field open
	The pass based on the identification of a free colleague

Task 2	
Goal	Passing actions with variation in the direction of the pass according to the position of the defender. The right and the left foot should be used accordingly.
Description	3 vs 1 participants distributed in a traingle with one participant acting as defender inside. The cones should be used as references for the reception and passing. If a pass is intercepted or a wrong pass occurs, the participant that loses the pass changes with the defender.
Feedback	Individual position before the moment of reception
	The use of different foot to receive the ball according to the cone, the passing direction and the defender displacement
	The individual reception of the ball opening the possibility to play to the left or to the right
	Pass velocity and precision according to the possision of the ball receiver and the defender

Task 3	
Goal	Ball possession between the attacking participants. The ball connot stop and the attackers should use the right and left foot accordingly the direction of the pass.
Description	3 vs 1 participants distributed in two sectors. In each sector there can only be two attackers. When the ball moves to the other sector the attacker defines if he moves to the other sector to support the ball carrier or not. If a pass is intercepted or a wrong pass occurs, the participant that loses the pass changes with the defender.
Feedback	Individual position before the moment of reception
	Where is the ball? How is your body position in relation to the ball and the other participants?
	What is the direction of displacement of the defender?
	How can you move to better receive the ball and open your possibilities of play?
	What is the precision of your pass?

Figure 7.1 Sequence of three tasks for developing passing actions in team sports.

Source: For each task, the goal, the description, and the feedback that coaches should use to highlight the main information and actions that individuals should follow are described.

different ball trajectories, receive the ball with both feet and effectively perform the pass with left or right foot according to pass direction. In the second task, the combination of the use of cones, the reduction in the number of possibilities for action and the presence of one opponent highlight passing lines and guide the participants to excel their spatial positioning, timing, and precision of actions with right and left foot (Figure 7.1, middle panel). In the third task a small sided and conditioned game includes the manipulation of the space of play and the numerical relation of participants to highlight how the passing actions can be explored in close connection with the opponent and teammates positions. The attacker with the ball needs to maintain a good spatial orientation and start to adjust his actions according to the movements of the defenders and attackers to explore passing actions in different directions to maintain ball possession (Figure 7.1, lower panel).

Self-processing questions

Box 7.6 A time to reflect – content review

- Which key principles of the CLA may underpin the design of learning environments?
- What is the role of constraints in shaping movement solutions at the ecological scale of individual-environment interaction?

Summary and key points

In this chapter we have covered the utility of adopting a CLA to the development of skill acquisition across different domains such as physical education and sport coaching. We highlighted the potential of selectively identifying and manipulating constraints in order to shape movement solutions across different sport games such as invasion, net-wall, and striking-fielding games. To ensure a desired level of coherence in the design of learning environments, the core principles that underpin CLA were thoroughly debated: *(i) preserving the integrity of perception-action coupling, (ii) implementing task simplification, (iii) promoting variability in learning contexts, and iv) favouring feedback with an external focus.* Exemplar tasks of a pedagogical progression in futsal were also provided as a means to empower sport educators to bridge the gap between theory and practice and design potentially challenging learning environments.

References

Barsingerhorn, A., Zaal, F., De Poel, H., & Pepping, G. (2013). Shaping decisions in volleyball an ecological approach to decision-making in volleyball passing. *International Journal of Sport Psychology, 44*(3), 197–214. doi: 10.7352/IJSP2013.44.197

Buzard, T., Farrow, D., Reid, M., & Masters, R. S. (2014). Modifying equipment in early skill development: A tennis perspective. *Research Quarterly for Exercise and Sport, 85*(2), 218–225. doi: 10.1080/02701367.2014.893054

Chow, J. Y., Davids, K., Hristovski, R., Araújo, D., & Passos, P. (2011). Nonlinear pedagogy: Learning design for self-organizing neurobiological systems. *New Ideas in Psychology, 29*, 189–200.

Coito, N., Davids, K., Folgado, H., Bento, T., & Travassos, B. (2020). Capturing and quantifying tactical behaviors in small-sided and conditioned games in soccer: A systematic review. *Research Quarterly for Exercise and Sport*. doi: 10.1080/02701367.2020.1823307

Davids, K., Button, C., & Bennett, S. (2008). *Dynamics of skill acquisition: A constraints-led approach*. Champaign: Human Kinetics Publishers.

Gray, R. (2020). Comparing the constraints led approach, differential learning and prescriptive instruction for training opposite-field hitting in baseball. *Psychology of Sport and Exercise, 51*, 101797. doi: 10.1016/j.psychsport.2020.101797

Newell, K. M. (1986). Constraints on the development of coordination. In M. Wade & H. T. A. Whiting (Eds.), *Motor development in children: Aspects of coordination and control* (pp. 341–360). Dordrecht: Martinis Nijhoff.

Paulo, A., Zaal, F., Fonseca, S., & Araújo, D. (2016). Predicting volleyball serve-reception. *Frontiers in Psychology, 7*, 1694.

Peh, S. Y.-C., Chow, J. Y., & Davids, K. (2011). Focus of attention and its impact on movement behaviour. *Journal of Science and Medicine in Sport, 14*(1), 70–78. doi: 10.1016/j.jsams.2010.07.002

Renshaw, I., Davids, K., Shuttleworth, R., & Chow, J. Y. (2009). Insights from ecological psychology and dynamical systems theory can underpin a philosophy of coaching. *International Journal of Sport Psychology, 40*, 580–602.

Sarmento, H., Clemente, F. M., Harper, L. D., Costa, I. T. d., Owen, A., & Figueiredo, A. J. (2018). Small sided games in soccer–a systematic review. *International Journal of Performance Analysis in Sport, 18*(5), 693–749. doi: 10.1080/24748668.2018.1517288

Sgrò, F., Bracco, S., Pignato, S., & Lipoma, M. (2018). Small-sided games and technical skills in soccer training: Systematic review and implications for sport and physical education practitioners. *Journal of Sports Science, 6*, 9–19. doi: 10.17265/2332-7839/2018.01.002

Sullivan, M. O., Woods, C. T., Vaughan, J., & Davids, K. (2021). Towards a contemporary player learning in development framework for sports practitioners. *International Journal of Sports Science & Coaching*, 17479541211002335. doi: 10.1177/17479541211002335

Timmerman, E., De Water, J., Kachel, K., Reid, M., Farrow, D., & Savelsbergh, G. (2015). The effect of equipment scaling on children's sport performance: the case for tennis. *Journal of Sports Sciences, 33*(10), 1093–1100. doi: 10.1080/02640414.2014.986498

Additional resources

https://perceptionaction.com/.
https://myfastestmile.com/category/ecological-dynamics/.

8 Creative Learning Activities
Thinking and Playing "Outside the Box"

*José Afonso, Ana Ramos, Patrícia Coutinho,
Cristiana Bessa, Isabel Mesquita,
Filipe Manuel Clemente, and Cláudio Farias*

Box 8.1 Objectives

At the end of this chapter, you will be able to:

- Understand the importance of developing creativity into the goals and learning task designs.
- Scaffold the learners' creativity from the micro-level to the meta-level.
- Design goal-based criteria as the core principle to progress or regress the learning tasks.
- Comprehend how variability can support the development of learners' creativity.

Box 8.2 Key sections

- Introduction
- A multilevel framework for developing creativity
- Practical tasks for creativity development

Introduction

In sport, creativity refers to the learners' ability to perform original and flexible decisions and actions that suddenly change the game flow to overcome the opponents within unexpected play situations (Memmert & Roth, 2007). The development of creativity is closely

DOI: 10.4324/9781003140016-11

linked with the appropriateness-based principles presented in Chapter 6, since improving creativity benefits from the ability to design and participate in learning tasks appropriate to each individual. As highlighted in Chapter 7, the principles of a constraints-led approach can be valuable to implement the premises of *appropriateness*, contributing to enhance learners' creativity. To exemplify, the manipulation of task constraints helps to develop learners' participation in shifting game-play environments that call for novel actions from players (i.e., differential learning; Schöllhorn, Hegen, & Davids, 2012).

Accordingly, our creativity-driven approach draws on the notion of representativeness (Chapter 6), to consider learning tasks that respect features of the formal game, while reconciling them with individual and societal-based goals (Le Noury, Buszard, Reid, & Farrow, 2021). Keeping in mind the promotion of creative actions throughout learners' development (Griggs & McGregor, 2012), we propose four levels of creativity development: micro-, meso-, macro-, and meta-level. Learners can move from a micro-level of creativity, in which they raise creative actions performing the role of players, to a meta-level where creativity is used to establish links between the sport and wider societal culture. The learners' creativity evolves through the combination of horizontal and vertical progressions (Rink, French, Werner, Lynn, & Mays, 1992) – see Chapter 6 for more details – over the four levels.

During the creativity developmental path, sport educators need to apply scaffolding strategies such as described in Chapters 3 and 4. Moreover, our proposal highlights the progressive sharing of responsibility between sport educators and learners, with accountability criteria bridging this relationship. For instance, at a meso-level, sport educators define the learning goal, but the task is designed by learners who establish individualized score systems that determines when the task/learning goal is achieved. Hence, this proposal is compatible with a gradual shift of responsibility to the learners in their active construction of game-based learning experiences through peer-teaching and collaborative interactions (see Chapters 4 and 6).

A multilevel framework for developing creativity

Conceptual principles

Creativity has been increasingly acknowledged as a core educational goal (Henriksen, Richardson, & Shack, 2020). In sport, however, it remains unclear what creativity is and how sport educators can facilitate its development in learners. The Oxford Learner's Dictionaries define creativity as "the use of skill and imagination to produce something new or to produce art".[1] This beautifully synthetic definition has several implications. On the one hand, creativity is limited by the skill set: learners can only create within their current level of skills; otherwise, creativity may become pointless, without actual implementation. For instance, every skilled skateboarder first had to learn how to perform simple balance tasks. Therefore, we advise readers to check the scaffolding strategies addressed in the previous chapters of this book. On the other hand, our definition of creativity suggests that when learners are equipped with a given set of skills, imagination can flow and learners may devise novel forms and contexts to apply such skills. We are not advocating that technique must be taught before game-play tactics; we are merely stating that decision-making and technique are deeply related and mutually sustain each other.

Learners may even imagine what extra skills should be developed (or what new games they can create; see Chapter 9) for putting into practice some creative thought they came up with. When implementing peer-coaching strategies, each learner may help other learners towards a faster, better, and more personalized process of game-play development (Quay & Peters, 2012). While skill development is considered in the planning of learning sessions, the evolving of imagination is often seen as a by-product or as attributable to some innate talent. Although we do not underestimate the concept of talent (whatever its meaning), we believe that everyone can *improve* their creativity. Big things have small beginnings, and sport educators should not expect creativity to emerge in full form. Instead, creativity slowly develops into broader and better-adjusted forms, but at different rates and timings for each learner.

As defined in Chapter 7, manipulating task constraints is an important component for designing appropriate learning tasks. Within each level, task constraints can be either relaxed or tightened (Hristovski, Davids, Araujo, & Passos, 2011). Simplifying the constraints (or level of explicit scaffolding) provides more degrees of freedom to learners and may promote creativity; however, if excessive degrees of freedom are available considering the learners' current level, creative actions may be inhibited due to an information overload. Conversely, constraints that are too tight afford little creativity, but they might play an important pedagogical role at specific moments (e.g., when learners have low background experience and need more explicit support; see Chapter 3). Tight constraints provide learners with the opportunity to increase the frequency of practice of novel and/or difficult skills within diversified learning scenarios. The challenge is to find a balance in sampling and manipulating the *appropriate constraints* adjusting them to the learners' level and pushing them a bit beyond that level (not too easy, not too difficult, "just right"). Of course, aligned with an appropriateness-based framework, this adjustment will be an ongoing and individualized process.

Designing creativity into the form of goals and learning activities is challenging. Sport activities may start by simplifying the learning scenarios and create a learning environment that promotes and values creative approaches (Deng, Zheng, & Chen, 2020). By default, this implies that *errors* made by learners are perceived as valuable learning opportunities. Overly punishing environments, where errors are discouraged (explicitly or implicitly) will invite learners to "play safe" and stay within their comfort zones. From our viewpoint, nothing novel or creative will emerge unless sport educators challenge and push learners towards the unknown, while still engaged within a risk-free and safe environment (i.e., where learners can experiment and fail without public embarrassment or punishment). Afterwards, sport educators can move on to design learning activities that promote exploratory actions and encourage learners to devise novel solutions to the presented situations (Hristovski et al., 2011).

Micro-level: game-specific creativity

Perhaps the most common use of creativity in the learning processes: here, sport educators establish the goals and design the tasks but afford some degree of exploratory game-play. A problem is presented, and learners can solve it through diverse ways, stimulating their creativity. Learners' peer-coaching may be more easily implemented at this level as learners will collaborate in reference to explicit goals and expectations placed by sport educators.

Although this micro-level is important, an excessive focus on this level may hold back the learners' progression along their creativity pathway. Eventually, game-based tasks can be proposed to offer specific constraints so that learners can promote divergent or convergent solutions. Nonetheless, constraints must allow learners to explore the dynamic environment and solve the problems based on their perceptions, resonating with the concept of *repetition without repetition* (Bernstein, 1967). Acknowledging the variability inherent to each action, learners are invited to explore and create different solutions under similar game-problems.

Meso-level: task-design creativity

What if sport educators provide the learners with the goals for a given game problem, but the learners themselves had to design the learning activity or task? This could provide an interesting challenge, whereby learners engage in transforming a learning goal into a practical application by designing a learning task. This process should be scaffolded (for example, through guided task design, guided task presentation or during peer-coaching pre-session briefings; see Chapters 3 and 4). When learners can successfully design their own tasks (see Chapter 9), they will have grasped the complexities of matching task conditions with the movement and tactical actions that these tasks promote (i.e., a deeper understanding of game concepts, cues perception, and decision-making processes; Memmert, 2015). Learners are likely to become more deeply committed to their learning experiences at this point. By placing the learner at the core of this process, since the tasks are designed by themselves to fit their own needs, the meso-level of creativity would expand the meaning of *appropriateness* of the learning experience (Chapter 6).

Macro-level: goal-setting creativity

What if learners were actively involved in setting their own goals? Such commitment would make the learners even more engaged with the process and development of an intensified sense of ownership of their learning experiences. Furthermore, the goal-setting would appeal to engage the learners in negotiation and in collaborative decision-making. Depending on where learners sit in their ability to take on leadership of instructional processes or, for example, the complexity level of the sport content being addressed (see the principle of "Contingency" in Chapter 3), this macro-level can be implemented in two ways (not mutually exclusive). On some occasions, the learners would be responsible for setting the learning goals, and afterwards the sport educator would design an appropriate learning task. On other occasions, the learners could both set the learning goals and design the appropriate learning tasks.

Meta-level: the role of creativity in bridging sport and society

Sport provides a powerful context to explore ever-evolving societal expectations, dilemmas, and challenges, and may be used to improve society itself. At the highest point of the educational impact of youth participation in sport, the development of sportpersons with a healthy sporting culture would result in a healthier, more democratic, and socially just society. The notion of transformation (Farias, Wallhead, & Mesquita, 2020) is paramount, as the humanistic values that are promoted through sport should not be restricted to the specific context of Physical Education (PE) or youth sport settings but applied and extended to broader societal contexts. The same is true when sport educators seek to assign augmented cultural, personal, and social meaning to learners' participation in the sport and game-based activities they promote (Eisenberg, Levin, & Eben, 2005).

The meta-level is where creativity fully allows sport to enhance human potential and provide a true transdisciplinary contribution (Vaughan, Mallett, Davids, Potrac, & López-Felip, 2019). Here, the learners became more socially aware human beings through participation in sport and the youngsters feel an embodied drive to actively participate in building a better society. This meta-level incorporates sociocultural constraints into sport while, at the same time, using sport to improve society. Ultimately, we believe that PE and youth sport should always (re)connect human and societal development which requires a creative collaborative approach (Kim et al., 2019). Some considerations:

- The first facet of meta-level creativity could present challenges to learners such as "For this specific goal, should we integrate the lower- with the higher-skilled learners, or separate the levels?"; "Why integrate or separate?"; and further, "How to balance integration and division by skills levels to promote learning while keeping a sense of unity?".
- The second facet of meta-level creativity could ask learners "What have we learned today [in the session] that can be applied to our daily lives?"; "What principles of citizenship can you derive from today's lesson?"; "How do you intend to apply this outside of the lesson?". At a certain point, perhaps even assume bolder choices and challenge the learners "How can we use sport to improve our school/community/city or even our understanding of others' actions/feelings?". At this point, the sport educator can prepare learners to be active facilitators in the promotion of sport events or to create projects that actively use sport to promote societal changes (for example, in their wider school or club context; Figure 8.1).

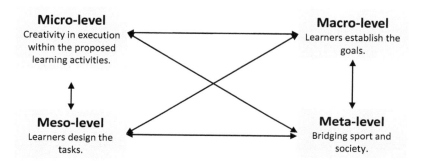

Figure 8.1 Levels of creativity built-in into the learning goals and activities.

Practical tasks for creativity development

The four domains of creativity are visited in the series of practical tasks offered below in Box 8.3–8.6.

Practical example 1: micro-level, game-play creativity

Suppose that during basketball game-play, the sport educator observes that lower-skilled learners are not able to dribble the ball forward every time an opponent pressures them in the central court lane. Learners pass the ball back to the defensive sector cutting off the attack flow. The sport educator understands that such action occurs due to the poor ability to dribble the ball and/or perform different types of passing. Accordingly, the sport educator splits the class into high- and low-skilled groups with both groups performing the same learning tasks, but with different accountability criteria per group. In doing so, the sport educator is providing learners with opportunities to create solutions adjusted to their skills.

Box 8.3 Task: seeking individual solutions

TASK: 2v1 game-form.

TACTICAL PROBLEM: Dribble the ball back when facing opponent pressure.

LEARNING GOAL: Dribble the ball in different ways, perform different passing.

SETTING: Class divided into two heterogeneous groups (lower- and higher-skilled).

TASK CONSTRAINT (STEP 1): Learners can (i) dribble the ball freely, scoring two-points, or (ii) pass the ball forward to a teammate, scoring one point.

TASK CONSTRAINT (STEP 2): Learners from lower-skilled group can only perform three ball contacts, while higher-skilled learners can only perform two ball contacts.

ACCOUNTABILITY CRITERIA: Lower-skilled group, to achieve five points; higher-skilled group, to achieve seven points.

If learners successfully perform the learning task, a progression could be the building of heterogeneous groups (i.e., evenly composed of higher- and lower-skilled learners). Indeed, as learners of different skill levels interact collaboratively to meet the task goals (especially if supported by group reflection problem-solving)[2] this can prompt the emergence of novel and innovative solutions for the task.

Practical example 2: meso-level, task-design creativity

Suppose there was a formal assessment moment of learners' football game-play and that the sport educator video-recorded this training session or PE lesson. The sport educator edits the video and deliberately analyses with learners some of their most recurring game problems. The constructive and collaborative discussion among sport educator and learners identifies that the team in ball possession struggles to create space, while the off-the-ball team is not closing space efficiently. Thus, the sport educator sets two learning task goals, and each group is invited to design a learning task that addresses the targeted game problems. After a while, each group proposes a learning task that is debated among all. When all the learning tasks were presented, debated and a consensus reached, all groups conduct the designed tasks, which after its practice can be adjusted, if necessary.[3]

Box 8.4 Task: designing tasks

TACTICAL PROBLEM: Create space in ball possession.
GAME-PLAY GOAL: (i) Create space in ball possession; (ii) close space and protect the goal when off-the-ball.
SETTING: Class divided into four groups.
TASK: Learners must design a learning task that addresses the tactical problem identified.

Practical example 3: macro-level, goal-setting creativity

Still within the football teaching, the sport educator collects video recordings of the performance of learners in the tasks designed by themselves and initiate the debate among the class by questioning learners about their opinions (see an example of questioning and hints that might fit here in Chapter 4: Discovery-based instruction-questioning and hints). Some of these questions might look like: "In ball possession, did you create space?"; "Did you see many attempts to goal?"; Through these questions, learners understand that they can now open or close space depending on if they have or not the ball possession, but they display difficulties in shooting. Thus, learners begin to grasp that the next challenge is related to designing and performing a learning task targeted deliberately for improving their shooting skills.

Box 8.5 Task: creating a new task

TACTICAL PROBLEM: Create opportunities for shooting.
LEARNING GOAL: (i) Create space in ball possession, and (ii) close space in off-the-ball situations
SETTING: Class divided into heterogeneous groups (higher- and lower-skilled learners).
TASK: 1v1 cooperative learning task.
TASK CONSTRAINT: (i) Two ball contacts maximum, (ii) the type of shooting must be different at each trial (e.g., left foot, right foot, inside of the foot, outside of the foot).
ACCOUNTABILITY CRITERIA: Five different goal shoots.

By adding these task constraints (i.e., number of contacts and type of shooting), the sport educator is redirecting the learners' attention, from a cognitive and motor perspective, to explore different solutions to accomplish the purpose, i.e., to score a goal. The learning task purpose is only reached when learners perform at least five different goal shoots (accountability criteria). Thus, the sport educator is promoting the action variability on shooting, inducing creativity development.

As the task is successfully accomplished, the teacher questions learners on how to progress the learning task. In doing so, the teacher is stimulating the learners' reflexive thinking, engaging them with their own learning process. The learners suggest introducing a goalkeeper and an opponent, thereby move to a 2v1 game-form against goalkeeper. The teacher redefines the task constraints, removing the limit of contacts but emphasizing the type of shooting, for instance, head or heel shooting doubles the score.

Practical example 4: meta-level, creativity bridging sport-to-society

The first side of the meta-level of creativity was addressed in the abovementioned examples through the integration or grouping of learners into homogeneous or heterogeneous groups. Thereby, we will focus on the second component of this meta-level: bridging PE content and the impact of the learners' holistic development on society. In this respect, more than the structure or content of the learning task, how sport educators define the task goals is vital. In fact, when sport educators define task goals focused on performance outcomes (e.g., score five points, repeat an action 15 times, perform a ten-minutes task) the quality of teaching-learning process is mostly focused on the class or training context. However, when sport educators define task goals based on processes (e.g., create space with ball possession score one point, award the most creative shooting) the teaching-learning process may be largely extended to outside of the PE content.

For example, a key strategy for extending learner participation in personally relevant sport experiences is the opportunity to connect experiences lived in PE or at the sport club with their lives outside these contexts. Sport educators should establish an authentic bridge between learners' sporting experiences and the "cultural world" in which they live in (their representations of sport). In the coaching setting, for example, the active inclusion of families in the athlete's sporting life is, increasingly, an unavoidable (and desirable) reality. It is up to the sport educator to positively manage this process. The following strategies are suggested.

***Establish links between the learning context and
the sport culture outside the institution***

Assigning extra learning "tasks" to learners, pending they do not become a "burden" for the youngster, can encourage learners to add meaning to their sport participation. Box 8.6 provides an example.

Box 8.6 Task: extending the learning experience

Sport educators inform learners about relevant sporting events (at other institutions, television events about adult versions of the sport, National team events related to different sports, etc.), holding them accountable (at different complexity/progressive levels) for reporting what they have learned with the experience: "Next session, I want you to tell me who the team's opponent was"; "Who was the best scorer?"; "How many saves did the goalkeeper make?"; "What tactical system did they play on?"; "Tell me an offensive strategy that we can apply in our own team and why".

***Establish links between the sport participation context and the
learner's family and social life***

Linking sport and social life is is about encouraging the learner to be an active mediator of the (positive) involvement of their family members in sports life (see Box 8.7).

Box 8.7 Task: linking sport and family lives

The practitioner is tasked for:

• Learning important facts about sport (e.g., questioning a grandfather about a prominent player of his time and carrying out, with supervision, the search in the usual sources of information).
• Bring family members to attend sporting events.
• Present proposals that align with the content requested by the coach (e.g., "We want to work on scoring play situations. Can you ask a more experienced friend or family member for some tips?").
• Find out about sporting events or local infrastructure (fitness-friendly parks, gyms, running, and charity events) where it is feasible to practice sport (e.g., during the season break).

Self-processing questions

Box 8.8 A time to reflect – content review
- What are the four levels at which creativity may operate?
- How can sport educators help learners design appropriate tasks?
- How can sport educators scaffold pedagogical processes so that learners become skilled in designing their own learning goals?
- How can sport educators develop the meta-level of creativity?

Summary and key points

This chapter presented four levels for promoting creativity: (i) micro-level (creativity in game actions within the proposed learning activities); (ii) meso-level (learners design the tasks); (iii) macro-level (learners establish the goals); and (iv) meta-level (bridging sport and society). Sport educators must identify the dynamics that emerge from the application of task constraints and promote creativity while guiding the learner through the learning process. The sensitivity to navigate across the levels is a challenge, considering they can be used within or between sessions. Peer-teaching should be implemented at all stages, in a scaffolded process (Chapters 3 and 4), towards ever-greater autonomous learning. Creativity-based proposals should also incorporate the concepts of appropriateness (Chapter 6) and constraints-led approach (Chapter 7).

Notes

1 Last consulted on November 27, 2021.
2 See "Reflective group discussions" in Chapter 3.
3 Sport educators can use pre-lesson briefings (see Chapter 3) to engage learners in the creation of their tasks. They can scaffold their built task conditions on prior tasks presented by the sport educator. Learners are guided to test how the task conditions prompt (or not) the emergence of the tactical actions they are looking for.

References

Bernstein, N. A. (1967). *The coordination and regulation of movements*. Oxford: Pergamon Press.

Deng, Q., Zheng, B., & Chen, J. (2020). The relationship between personality traits, resilience, school support, and creative teaching in higher school physical education teachers. *Frontiers in Psychology, 11*, 2397. doi: 10.3389/fpsyg.2020.568906

Farias, C., Wallhead, T., & Mesquita, I. (2020). "The project changed my life": Sport education's transformative potential on student physical literacy. *Research Quarterly for Exercise and Sport, 91*(2), 263–278. doi: 10.1080/02701367.2019.1661948

Griggs, G., & McGregor, D. (2012). Scaffolding and mediating for creativity: Suggestions from reflecting on practice in order to develop the teaching and learning of gymnastics. *Journal of Further and Higher Education, 36*(2), 225–241. doi: 10.1080/0309877X.2011.614929

Henriksen, D., Richardson, C., & Shack, K. (2020). Mindfulness and creativity: Implications for thinking and learning. *Thinking Skills and Creativity, 37*, 100689. doi: 10.1016/j.tsc.2020.100689

Hristovski, R., Davids, K., Araujo, D., & Passos, P. (2011). Constraints-induced emergence of functional novelty in complex neurobiological systems: A basis for creativity in sport. *Nonlinear Dynamics-Psychology and Life Sciences, 15*(2), 175–206.

Kim, Y. E., Morton, B. G., Gregorio, J., Rosen, D. S., Edouard, K., & Vallett, R. (2019). Enabling creative collaboration for all levels of learning. *Proceedings of the National Academy of Sciences, 116*(6), 1878–1885. doi: 10.1073/pnas.1808678115

Le Noury, P., Buszard, T., Reid, M., & Farrow, D. (2021). Examining the representativeness of a virtual reality environment for simulation of tennis performance. *Journal of Sports Sciences, 39*(4), 412–420. doi: 10.1080/02640414.2020.1823618

Memmert, D., & Roth, K. (2007). The effects of non-specific and specific concepts on tactical creativity in team ball sports. *Journal of Sports Sciences, 25*(12), 1423–1432. doi: 10.1080/02640410601129755

Rink, J. E., French, K. E., Werner, P. H., Lynn, S., & Mays, A. (1992). The influence of content development on the effectiveness of instruction. *Journal of Teaching in Physical Education, 11*(2), 139. doi: 10.1123/jtpe.11.2.139

Schöllhorn, W. I., Hegen, P., & Davids, K. (2012). The nonlinear nature of learning - A differential learning approach. *The Open Sports Sciences Journal, 5*(Suppl.1-M11), 100–112.

Vaughan, J., Mallett, C. J., Davids, K., Potrac, P., & López-Felip, M. A. (2019). Developing creativity to enhance human potential in sport: A wicked transdisciplinary challenge. *Frontiers in Psychology, 10*, 2090. doi: 10.3389/fpsyg.2019.02090

Additional Resources

Eisenberg, J., Levin, M., & Eben, M. (2005). *Creativity in sport: The triumph of imagination*. Toronto, Canada: Chestnut Pub Group.

Memmert, D. (2015). *Teaching tactical creativity in sport. Research and practice*. Routledge.

9 Learner-Designed Games

The Ultimate Empowerment of Sport Learners

Peter A. Hastie

Box 9.1 Objectives

At the end of this chapter you will be able to:

- Identify the advantages of having learners design their own games
- Define a good game
- Understand the game design process
- Appreciate the role of the sport educators and learners in the games-making process

---

Box 9.2 Key sections

- Introduction
- Defining games
- Structuring the games-making experience
- Practical tasks

Introduction

Games with rules are a uniquely human form of play. While most animal species engage in playful activity, it is only humans who introduce rules that limit certain possibilities. In football, you cannot carry the ball in your hands. In a running race you need to stay in a particular lane (where it would be quicker to run across the infield). Yet this is not the reason that we play games. Put most simply "playing a game is the voluntary attempt to overcome unnecessary obstacles" (Suits, 1978, p. 41).

DOI: 10.4324/9781003140016-12

When students design their own games, and sport educators allow young people the chance to negotiate games and their rules rather than performing already learned techniques, we position game-play as an even impressive intellectual (and creative) operation (Kretchmar, 2007).

It is the purpose of this chapter to describe the processes and mechanisms that help young people in Physical Education (PE) and sport settings to design their own games. As Mauldon and Redfern (1969), as well as Riley (1975) have commented, to be involved in a game, to decide upon the rules, to find answers to problems that arise and ultimately to play a mutually designed game, challenges students to use their inventiveness and creativity "to devise their own activities in which the need for rules arises naturally" (1969, p. 17). More recent studies have shown that game design helps students to not only practice specific skills but provide a forum that allows students to develop a more sophisticated understanding of game structures and game-play (Casey, Hastie, & Rovegno, 2011). Both of these are valuable outcomes in PE and youth sport settings.

Defining games

What is a game?

One of the first activities that sport educators need to address with their learners is to discuss what makes a game, "a game". This is valuable as most young people have almost exclusive experience as "players", rather than designers. As such, they have participated in games where the rules and limits are presented to them, rather than being in the position where they make these decisions.

In essence, players in a game are trying to achieve a specific goal or objective (known as "how to win"). If there is one thing every game needs, it is a clear objective: survive to the end, be the first to finish, or to get the most points. The objective of any good game must be clear, concise, intuitive, and memorable. It should also be at the top of the rulebook in paragraph number one. In meeting the goal however, games players are allowed to use only means permitted by rules (what you are allowed to do). Further, there are a number of limitations of these permitted means (What you are *not* allowed to do).

Take football as an example. The objective is to get a ball into your opponent's goal more often than they do. The means for getting the ball into the goal are limited to striking it with one's feet or head. Players can move the ball up field by dribbling or passing, and are allowed to directly intercept these movements and to dispossess an opponent.

Nonetheless, players are *not* allowed to carry the ball with their hands (and hence they cannot throw it to a partner or into the goal), and they are *not* allowed to dispossess an opponent using physical contact that might be allowed in rugby. Finally, players are limited to certain spaces on the field in relation to the location of the ball and their opponents.

What is a "good" game?

When introducing game design to young people, it is important to discuss what constitutes a "good game". Table 9.1 lists a number of characteristics that make up "good", which in most cases, translates to "fun". However, primary among these is that the game must "work".

For a game to work, it *must* be possible to achieve the goal. In some cases, the rules advantage the defense so much that scoring becomes almost impossible. In others, there are so many options for scoring that it's almost impossible to defend. This is not only the case in invasion games like football or basketball, but also in batting and fielding games or in target games.

The second element of games that is strongly valued by young people lies in their ability to involve all the players most of the time. As Kramer (2015) notes, nothing kills players' interest as easily as long periods of inactivity while they wait for their turns. Further, all players should be involved in the game until it is almost over. No one should be eliminated until the very end.

In addition to these, it is particularly important in education settings such as PE and youth sport, that the game is "safe". By safe, we mean the game not only has rules that keep its participants physically safe, but that there are no opportunities for learners to be embarrassed or humiliated.

Table 9.1 Components of good games

Components of good games
• **continuous challenges** – each challenge leads to another challenge
• **many different ways to accomplish each goal** – each player (or team) can work out their own strategy
• **easy to learn yet hard to master** – clear and simple rules, but skills need time to master
• **original** – it has to possess elements that have never, or at least not in this particular combination, been part of a game before
• **freshness and replayability** – is different as possible each time it is played
• **clear performance criteria** – to let players know how well or poorly they are doing

How do sport learners design their games?

Research on games-making has shown a few trends that sport educators might wish to consider as they ask their apprentices to create new games. First, some learners (particularly girls and lower-skilled players), tend to fully plan their games on paper, attempting to consolidate all the constitutive rules before they engage in play (Hastie & André, 2012). Girls tend to be more likely to change their games more frequently.

Others (particularly boys and higher-skilled players) tend to start from a basic idea of a game's goals and then tinker with rules and experiment as they play. They typically discuss one or two ideas and start testing them within a few minutes of receiving the assignment. Further, higher-skilled boys can often sometimes detect issues with a game without even playing it. Lower-skilled learners often struggle to see potential problems with their games (Hastie & André, 2012).

Structuring the games-making experience

Games-making is not simply a case of telling sport learners to "make up a game". Many young people do not understand the reason for rules and the ways rules affect game-play. Sometimes they do not understand how to change a rule to make the game fairer.

Box 9.3 Key point: two parts scaffolding of the games-making experience

1   Sport educators first make decisions about the goal of the experience, the type of game they want learners to design, and the structure of the learning groups.
2   The sport learners and sport educators then interact using a form of "design – play – revise" cycle to come up with their final games.

Part 1 - Sport educator decisions prior to student involvement

What is the goal of the games-making experience?

There are a number of different goals obtainable from games-making, and it is valuable for sport educators to consider which of these would be the focus of the student experience. Some of these include:

- Discovering why rules are important and what purpose they serve
- Creating completely new games
- Sharing ideas and working cooperatively
- Teaching others
- Actively engaging with and exploring components of game-play (skills and strategy)
- Thinking critically about games experiences outside of class and school
- Practicing specific elements of a game

As can be seen, some goals focus more on the "understanding" (i.e., cognitive) aspects of games playing, such as "how rules determine the tactics that are used". Others are more oriented to affective and youth development outcomes. Still others are designed to help improve player motor skill performance.

What type of game should be made?

Once the objective of the experience is determined, the sport educator needs to decide upon the type of game and the extent of learner choice. From experience, games can be placed into three groups, based upon the level of interaction between players (both within and across teams), as well as the number of variables that need to be managed by the participants. As a result, sport learners may need more overall sporting exposure before being able to master the design process in invasion games compared with tag games. Table 9.2 shows this differentiation.

Allocating students to groups

Given that game design is a collective process, participants need to be allocated into small learning groups. These need to be large enough so ideas can be shared, but not so large that some learners are unheard. Groups of about 4 or 5 seem to be more effective.

It is not necessary to ensure all groups have equal games playing ability. Some of the most creative ideas come from less experienced or

Table 9.2 Level of interaction and variability within games

Lower		Higher
Target games	Tag games	Invasion games
Net/wall games	Striking/fielding games	

less skilful games players. One reason for this is that they do not come to the games-making process with traditional ideas of how sports should be played. What the most skilful players do add, however, is the ability to detect any rules that would make the game unbalanced or could make a game break down.

Part 2 - The games-making process

Effective games-making sport educators follow a four-stage game design process, where they gradually scaffold the experience of "playing" into one where learners develop understanding through playing and modifying. These stages are listed as follows: (i) presenting the challenge, (ii) planning, (iii) playing and evaluating, (iv) revising and finalizing.

Presenting the challenge

Once learners have been allocated to design groups, the sport educator will present the task. If the challenge is to design a simple modified game challenge (e.g., a quick game that focuses on defending a corner in football), it is usually sufficient to present the task verbally. However, if the situation calls for learners to design a completely new game, having a written script (or template) is helpful. The text by Hastie (2010) has design templates for games from all the major categories. Table 9.3 provides a sample for the design of a target game, together with the choices of the learners.

Allowing time to plan

Learners need time to think and explore different options when they begin to design games. As they work through the challenge, and particularly as they try to fit together parts of more complex games, they will see that certain changes need to be made to their original ideas. It is important not to rush the process of the initial design. As noted earlier in this chapter, some learners prefer to have all their ideas about the goals and rules of a game before they start to play. Others will begin by playing a skeleton form of their game, and then make modifications as they face challenges.

Providing time for playing

While teams will play parts of their games during the design process, most games require more players and will thereby need the

Table 9.3 Target game template

Target game			
A	*?*	*Possible choices*	*Which did you choose?*
Target	What is the target	Hoop Pin Box Ball Marked area	Two large bowling pins standing back to back
	Where is the target	On the ground In the air Standing up	It is on the floor, after a narrow tunnel formed by 10 smaller pins
	How far is the target	Distance How do you mark the distance	The large pins are 3m from the first bowling line, and 5m from the second line. All players have a free choice as to which line to bowl from.
B	*?*	*Possible choices*	*Which did you choose?*
Goal of the game	What is the goal of the game?	Get the highest points by hitting the target with the highest values Hit the most targets Be the closest to the target Take the fewest turns to hit all the targets	Each large pin knocked down counts for 5 points. Each small pin counts as a 1-point deduction from the total. If you bowl from the second (more distant) line, all points are doubled.
C	*?*	*Possible choices*	*Which did you choose?*
Object	What do you send to the target?	Light ball Heavy ball Bean bag Horseshoe Foam javelin Something else	A heavy solid ball about 15cm in diameter.
	How do you send the object?	Underhand toss Overhand throw Push Strike Other form of release	The ball must be rolled underhand.

Target game

D	?	*Possible choices*	*Which did you choose?*
Scoring	How do you determine who wins?	Add the scores from each player for a team total. Players go head to head and add total wins.	Each player on a team bowls one time until all the bowled. Then the second team has its turn. Game designers decide on the number of players on each team and the number of rounds.
E	?	*Options*	*What is your choice?*
Obstacles	Are there penalties or obstacles?	Miss a turn Add a turn (as a penalty) Add or subtract points	Each small time that is knocked down results in a loss of 1 or 2 points, depending on the original bowling line.

participation of other teams. It is important to allow learners to see their game being played. When other teams play their game, the design team will get a better insight into their game. Players from other teams might find new strategic answers to the games' challenges, and they may also find loopholes in the rules (or at least some confusion about the intent of the rules). Hastie (2010) suggests this confusion can be caused by three situations: first, the game was poorly explained; second, the presenting team officiates the game poorly; and third, when a situation arises in a game for which no rule has yet been established. However, the process of fine-tuning and learning about games that comes from playing far outweighs the frustrations associated with game presentation.

Revising and finalizing the game

After teams have had the chance to see their games being played, they can decide to refine existing rules or perhaps introduce new rules aimed at countering or accommodating tactical solutions they had not foreseen. They may also make changes to the dimensions of the playing area or the size of the scoring area (see Chapter 7). Once these are consolidated, the group members should record all game details (rules, equipment, boundaries, etc.) in a game-playbook.

Practical tasks

In practical terms, there are two ways in which sport leaders can focus the games-making process. These lie in what the sport learners are asked to do. These are: (i) modifying an existing game and (ii) designing a completely new game.

Modifying existing games

Playing the whole game but changes to secondary rules

Sport learners (particularly those in PE settings), can be asked to make changes to existing games with the goal of making them more inclusive, more developmentally appropriate, novel, or engaging. Learners are able to change the equipment, scoring, and other secondary rules, while maintaining the fundamental premise of the original game (i.e., retaining it as an invasion or net/wall game).

A good example of an adaption of basketball that is popular with learners is "Flickerball". Flickerball is played on a basketball court but uses an oval ball (such as an American football or rugby ball) instead of a basketball. Scoring is expanded depending upon what the offensive team can achieve. A made basket scores 3; a shot that hits the hoop but does not fall in scores 2; a ball that hits only the backboard scores 1.

Within this modification, learners can experiment with and decide upon the rules concerning possession and progression. A common possession rule is that if the ball is dropped it is turned over to the opposing team. A common progression rule is that players cannot move with the ball, and a common scoring rule is that all shots need to be made outside the free-throw area.

Designing game-like tasks (player-designed challenges)

In the coaching setting, the sport is already determined, and players spend limited time practicing each week. With respect to the first, it would not make a lot of sense for a group of basketball players to be asked to modify a batting and fielding game.

What is possible however, is that the sport leader asks players to design game-like tasks. These can be segments of a game that typically will serve to magnify a particular aspect of play that the sport educator wants to highlight. These game-like tasks can be presented as "player-designed challenges". The goals of these challenges can either be to (a) be the fastest to complete the challenge with no errors, or (b) to the most points from a specific number of trials. When helping young people to develop these player-designed challenges, it is helpful to introduce them to the three pedagogies outlined by Launder and Piltz (2013) in their text *Play Practice* (see Table 9.4).

The following game gives an example of all three of these within one game.

Table 9.4 Player-designed challenges

Strategies used in player-designed challenges	
Shaping games	Games are modified in terms of the number of players, the size of the field, the ratio of attackers to defenders, and the type of goal. These are common in football settings where players content 4v2 games, and score by passing to team mates in certain zones.
Focusing games	Emphasizing specific aspects of game play, such as changing the shape/dimensions of the playing area. In badminton, for example, the court might be marked to identify target zones. If the goal of the task is to force the opponent to move to the back of the court, points can be scored during the game if the shuttle lands in a particular marked area towards the back of the court.
Enhancing games	Either increases or decreases the challenge and difficulty of the play as it appears in the adult form. Examples, include having short game times (e.g. 2–3 minutes), establishing tasks that must be completed in a specified period of time (or within a specified number of attempts), and giving players particular roles (limits of what specific players can or cannot do).

Box 9.4 Task: sample game

THE GAME: The game is a 4 (attacking) versus 2 (defenders) +1 (goal-keeper) challenge in football [shaping].

HOW IT BEGINS: The ball starts as a free-kick outside the penalty box and the attacking team has five trials. The ball begins at a different place (chosen by the attackers) for each trial [focusing]. Before each free-kick, the defenders list one

(Continued)

attacking player who *cannot* score (but certainly can be part of the play) [enhancing].

WINNING: To win, this team must score three goals across its five opportunities. Likewise, the defenders win if they hold the attackers to two or fewer goals [enhancing]. Winning points are allocated to individual players, who then rotate to form new teams. After all players have rotated, there will be an individual with the highest score. Each opportunity ends with either a score, or with a save, loss of possession or the ball going out of play.

Designing a completely new game

When sport learners are charged with designing new games, they benefit significantly from having templates to work from. Table 9.3 presented such a template for target games. Three more are presented that address the key aspects that need to be considered for (i) striking/fielding, (ii) net/wall, and (iii) invasion games (Tables 9.5–9.7).

Table 9.5 A striking and fielding games design template

Striking and fielding game

Game component	Options
How do you score?	Hit over boundary
	Running to or past a point
	Running a pathway
How do you get "out"	Caught (what about off the wall?)
	Throw to base
	After a number of swings/attempts
	Tagged
	Obstructing fielders
	Hit with the ball
	Run out of area
	Bat out of area
What implements will be used?	Hand
	Foot
	Body
	Bat
	Paddle
	Racquet

Striking and fielding game

Game component	Options
How does the batter receive the ball?	Pitch to own team
	Pitch to opposition
	Pitch from a machine
	Toss to yourself
	Off a tee
	Off a bounce
Where do batters hit from?	From an end line hitting forward
	From two end lines
	From the middle of the field to anywhere
	From a corner
What is the shape of the field, and what are the boundaries?	Rectangle
	Fan
	Oval
	Boundaries or no?
	What about walls and ceilings?
When do teams change from batting to fielding?	Number of outs
	Time at bat
	After certain score
	After everyone bats
	After number of batters

Table 9.6 An invasion games design template

Invasion games design

Game component	Options
How do you score?	Goal (air or ground)
	Ball to person in a certain place
	Gain possession
	Move ball over a line
How can you progress up the court or field?	Pass
	Throw
	Run
	Push
	Strike
	Dribble
	Kick
	Ride
	Swim

(Continued)

Invasion games design

Game component	Options
What implement(s) are you going to use to move with?	Round ball
	Oval ball
	Puck
	Flag, sock, beanbag
	Person only
	Animal (simulated!)
	Various dense/size ball
	Stick to carry the ball
	Stick to hit the ball
How do you get possession?	After a score
	Interception
	Tackle or tag
	Fumble or strip
	Rebound
	Violation
	Out of play
	Opposition has no more turns
How do you start the game or begin a new period?	Tip off
	Face off
	Designated receiver
	Coin toss for possession
	Shoot off
What are the boundaries?	None
	Sidelines only
	Walled in
	Shape = various
What are the goals?	Size
	Shape
	Location
	Angle
	Number
How do you resume play following a score?	Simply continue – play does not stop
	Possession to opponent
	Jump ball
	Face off
	Throw in by referee
	Alternate possession
What are the consequences of rule violations?	Faults/penalties
	Break progression rule
	Break possession rule
	Break scoring rule

Table 9.7 A net-wall games design template

Sample net-wall game	
How many players?	3 vs. 3
How do you score?	Opponent fails to return the ball over the dead zone and into the court
Where does the ball travel?	Over a dead space – if the ball lands in the zone between the 2 courts, it is out (used instead of a net)
What implements and ball/object are used?	No implements, only body parts Large high bounce inflatable ball
How many touches and/or bounces are allowed?	Maximum of 2 bounces and 3 touches on each side The bounces and touches can be in any order as most appropriate. The same player may use consecutive touches.
How does the game or rally start?	The team who won the last rally serves underhand from a line 3m behind the dead zone.
What are the dimensions?	The court can be as long as the players choose (or have space). The width is very narrow (no more than 4m). There is a 4m space between the 2 courts (this is the dead zone). ** In one version of this game, a large wall served as one sideline. The ball could be played off the wall, and the wall could be used as a strategy.
What other faults or penalties are included?	The ball cannot be caught or thrown. It must be hit with a striking action.

Self-processing questions

Box 9.5 A time to reflect – content review

- The games-making process is aided when the sport leader has good content knowledge of the game form. How confident are you in being able to help scaffold learner's progression through the design and revision process?
- In what situations do you believe it might be better for the sport leader to allocate learners to design teams, and when to allow them to select their own?
- How many lessons or training sessions would you be prepared to allocate for games-making experiences?

Summary and key points

Games-making is a process in which learners create, organize, practice, and refine their own games within certain limits established by the sport educator. The type of game to be designed can be structured by the sport educator. They can range from an open-ended format, to the design of challenges aimed to improve skill performance or highlight a tactical principle. Sport learners' overall engagement is generally very high across all aspects of games-making. Further, they complete all their game design tasks without the need for any form of extrinsic motivation.

Games-making is an excellent forum for helping sport learners to demonstrate improved literacy. Through the process of game design and revision, they come to understand the overarching principles, rules, and structures of games, and appreciate their importance, and are able to transfer them from one game to another.

Non-skilful and less experienced games players are often empowered during games-making. This is because less constrained and perhaps less locked into traditional ideas, they provide a level of creativity and novelty into games. As a result, games that are designed may either be competitive, cooperative, or presented as skill/tactical challenges. The biggest challenge faced by learners lies in the desire to have a goal that makes things fun, new, and enjoyable, and the reality of developing a set of constitutive rules that make that goal possible.

References

Casey, A., Hastie, P. A., & Rovegno, I. (2011). Student learning during a unit of student-designed games. *Physical Education & Sport Pedagogy, 16*(4), 331–350. https://doi.org/10.1080/17408989.2011.557654

Hastie, P. (2010). *Student-designed games*. Champaign, IL: Human Kinetics.

Hastie, P. A., & André, M. H. (2012). Game appreciation through student designed games and game equipment. *International Journal of Play, 1*(2), 165–183.

Kramer, W. (2015). What makes a game good? *Game and Puzzle Design, 1*(2), 84–86.

Kretchmar, R. S. (2007). The normative heights and depths of play. *Journal of the Philosophy of Sport, 34*(1), 1–12. https://doi.org/10.1080/00948705.2007.9714705

Launder, A., & Piltz, W. (2013). *Play practice: The games approach to teaching and coaching sports*. Champaign, IL: Human Kinetics.

Mauldon, E., & Redfern, H. B. (1969). *Games teaching: A new approach for the primary school.* London: Macdonald & Evans.

Riley, M. (1975). Elementary games and humanism. *Journal of Physical Education and Recreation, 46*(2), 46–49.

Suits, B. (1978). *The grasshopper: Games, life and utopia.* Toronto: University of Toronto Press.

Additional resource

Video: student designed games (https://peandsportvlog.wordpress.com/2015/05/28/vlog-10-student-designed-games/).

Part IV

Learner-Oriented Assessment

10 Harmonizing the Teaching-Assessment-Learning Cycle

Patrícia Coutinho, José Afonso, Ana Ramos, Cristiana Bessa, Cláudio Farias and Isabel Mesquita

---

Box 10.1 Objectives

- Understand assessment as opportunities for learning and for guiding the teaching and learning process.
- Conceive of assessment and learning as two sides of the same coin.
- Establish links between teaching, learning, and assessment.
- Create tailor-made assessments that respect inter-individual and intra-individual variability.

Box 10.2 Key sections

- Introduction
- Teaching, assessing, and learning as interdependent processes
- Tailor-made assessment and learners' intra- and inter-individual variability
- Assessment interactions
- The timing of assessment
- Assessment and the responsive modification of learning goals and tasks.

Introduction

Learning is an active process that depends on inner transformations driven by the close engagement of learners with the subject matter of sport and games and processes of active learning (Entwistle, 2000). These transformations develop in a nonlinear fashion (i.e., with the same task

DOI: 10.4324/9781003140016–14

conditions promoting different movement outcomes in different learners) (Pinder, Davids, Renshaw, & Araújo, 2011) and are influenced by considerable inter-individual and intra-individual variability (e.g., age, experience, social environment; van de Rut & Grey, 2019). To cater for the personal attributes and developmental stages of each child, learning and assessment should be regarded as deeply related processes that respect the learning pathway of each learner together with the learning goals and instructional dynamics set by sport and games. In this sense, we advocate that an inclusive and equitable quality education requires the harmonizing of assessment, teaching, and learning. Therefore, we seek to demonstrate the application of more dynamical, open-ended learning goals and tailor-made assessment strategies that bring the learner to the core of the pedagogical experience of learning sport and games.

Teaching, assessing, and learning as interdependent processes

Commonly, assessment strategies – both in Physical Education (PE) and youth sport contexts – are highly standardized, favouring equality (i.e., one-size-fits-all approach) over equity (i.e., tailor-made approach) (SHAPE America - Society of Health and Physical Educators, 2014). Such uniformization facilitates the assessment process, reducing the complexity and inherent diversity of learners into a single set of (assumingly) common features. However, learners do not develop, learn, or interpret the same content and processes at the same pace and in the same way. The developmental process is subjected to considerable inter-individual and intra-individual differences. Therefore, it is unrealistic to predict the specific pattern of any learning process in terms of its direction (i.e., positive or negative), magnitude (i.e., high or low), and timings (i.e., fast or slow). In a learner-oriented approach, the principle of contingency (see Chapter 3) is also applicable to the dynamic relationship between instruction and assessment. Put simply, the effectiveness of instruction and learning goals (e.g., task modification and learning goals) should align thoroughly and possibly be evaluated by clear assessment processes (focus, timing) (Lund & Veal, 2013). In turn, such assessment should inform the next teaching steps (i.e., instruction and learning goals; Entwistle & Peterson, 2004). In this sense, sport educators need to adopt flexible, evolving planning and assessment protocols, capable of keeping pace with learners' responses to the activities. In other words, the assessment must be representative of what is taught (and intended to be learned), and the ways in which the sport content is taught must be contingently adjusted to the information drawn from the assessment.

In this perspective, learners can be assessed on different occasions and in reference to different learning contents (or the same contents, but under distinct sets of task conditions). Moreover, even when assessed in similar contents and timing, the form of the assessment can be adjusted considering learners' current skill level (Gardner, 2011). Thereby, learner-oriented assessment strategies require a tailor-made approach to the content, timings, and forms of assessment (Yell, Collins, Kumpiene, & Bateman, 2020). Learners should acknowledge the importance of their active role on their self-assessment and the peers' assessment in their learning process (see benefits of self- and peer-assessment in Chapter 12). So, assessment in a learner-oriented perspective takes into consideration the following premises (Figure 10.1):

- Each learning activity is an opportunity for assessment, and each assessment is also a learning opportunity, ensuring the ecological validity of learning-assessment. Failing to understand this concept results in wasting powerful opportunities to scaffold learners' development.
- If learning is viewed as dynamic, complex, and nonlinear, assessment must be seen with the same lenses. This implies that the scheduling, tools, goals, and protocols of assessment must be flexible and adapted over time, avoiding the application of overly standardized and rigid protocols.

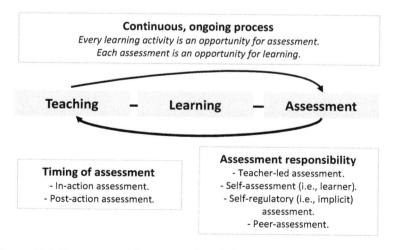

Figure 10.1 Dynamic and interdependent links between teaching, learning, and assessment.

– Ongoing assessments are opportunities to enrich the learning experience and should be a natural part of each, and every, learning activity. Learning assessments afford a singular opportunity to inform which problems related to the teaching-learning of sport and games need to be addressed in the subsequent pedagogical interventions (e.g., next class or training session), supporting how it could be operationalized (i.e., how learning tasks can be designed – task representativeness; Pinder et al., 2011). In this sense, assessment for marks should be understood as complementary and (perhaps) not the main concern of the learning process.

Tailor-made assessment and learners' intra- and inter-variability

When sport educators apply one-size-fits-all assessment they are mixing concepts such as equality and equity. Whereas equality is the promotion of equal treatment for every learner, equity is the promotion of differential treatment for each person. Equity is an attempt to being fair and impartial and to cater for the unique developmental path of each learner (Espinoza, 2007). Considering the different sporting background and experiences of each learner (e.g., motor strengths and limitations, personality, socio-cultural and family context), as well as their unique and innate potential, aiming for equality can in fact promote inequity in the participation opportunities of different learners. At worst, sport educators may be aspiring for learning outcomes that some learners are simply not prepared to deliver.

In this sense, individualized assessment criteria, or at least *more tailored assessment strategies*, could better address the issues of equity and fairness presented in pedagogical approaches that place the learner centre stage (López-Pastor, Kirk, Lorente-Catalán, MacPhail, & Macdonald, 2013). The concept of tailor-made assessment strategies may present itself in several different forms. A few key points and practical applications are provided in Box 10.3–10.6. The appropriateness principle is maintained in that task, goals and learners' responses progress interconnectedly (Chapter 6).

Box 10.3   Key point: assessing the same content, with similar task constraints, but adopting different assessment criteria

This is perhaps the easiest option to implement, even though also the most incomplete one, in our perspective. In this scenario, all learners are being assessed for the same learning contents and under the same task constraints. However, there are different sets of criteria for each group of learners, e.g., according to their skill level. This means that one group of learners will have to achieve a minimum assessment criterion, while other groups may be required to achieve a higher threshold.

Box 10.4 Key point: assessing the same learning content, but under different task constraints

Even if all learners are being assessed for the same learning contents, learners at different stages can be assessed through distinct task constraints. For example, while lower-skill learners may have to perform under relatively simple and/or stable conditions of practice, higher-skill learners may have to face harder and/or more unstable task constraints.

Box 10.5 Key point: assessment performed at different time points

Regardless of the learners being assessed for similar or dissimilar contents, and under similar or dissimilar task constraints, assessments may be performed in different timings. Some learners may be assessed earlier, as the teacher observes that the learner is reasonably proficient for being assessed and can move on to the next challenges. Conversely, other learners may benefit from spending more time in their current activities, in which case their assessments can be postponed.

Box 10.6 Task: assessing different content for different learners

If the age-old adage that "each person is unique" is to be taken seriously, then different learners have different personalities, skills, background, and contexts over time. Therefore, education should promote the diversity of learning contents, enriching them with relevant stimuli, instead of delivering the same curriculum to all learners. Moreover, recognizing that each learner has their own developmental path, it is important that each learner (or groups of learners) is assessed for different learning contents:

- Assessment of different learning contents from unrelated areas or themes (e.g., one learner is assessed in softball, while another is evaluated in netball).
- In basketball, some students are assessed on motor execution components (elbow and hand angle and movement during shooting actions) while other learners are being assessed on more complex tactical skills (using a screen move to create space in the attack).

Assessment interactions

In many PE and youth coach settings, sport educators lead and conduct the assessment process (Hay & Penney, 2014). In a learner-oriented approach, this is also legitimate. However, as sport educators feel more confident and pedagogically competent in transferring responsibility to the learners, it is expected that they involve learners more actively in the assessment moments.

Besides typical adult-led assessment, there are two additional features of assessment that can positively contribute to the learners' personal and social growth: self- and peer-assessment.

Self-assessment

The assessment perspective adopted in this chapter contrasts with the formal quantitative self-assessment used near the end of each school period. Self-assessment should not be a formality where learners state the grade that they believe is fair. Self-assessment should be imbued in the daily routines of education (see below, "Assessment and the responsive (contingent) modification of learning goals and tasks"). The ability to self-assess is a critical skill for personal human development. Like any other skill, it requires training, but what it develops is paramount for society. By engaging in self-assessment, the learners must progressively build a greater and more accurate self-awareness of their strengths and weaknesses. This, we believe, will provide the learner with a more precise notion of where they fit in each learning domain. Concurrently, it will promote the development of self-reflective skills which, in turn, expedites personal growth. Furthermore, the understanding of discrepancies between self-assessment and peer-assessment on their performance will afford a deeper comprehension of their conception of the *self* as well as more in-depth knowledge of one's own real abilities and limitations. Therefore, self-assessment should be intrinsic to all educational processes.

Peer-assessment

In the same view, learners should learn how to (fairly) assess their peers. Peer-assessment brings multiple advantages, namely:

- Each learner has access to more (and diversified) feedbacks, as the adult teacher or coach is now assisted by other "teachers" or "coaches"
- The learners in charge of peer-assessment activities; by itself, this strategy may facilitate learning through development of attentional focus and reflexive skills.
- Greater commitment to the learning activities – since all learners now also become "teachers", they will likely be more deeply invested into the common project.
- Superior self-awareness – by teaching their peers, each learner will inevitably develop a higher sense of what is required in each learning activity; as the learners are assessing their peers, they will simultaneously become more self-aware (Hwang, Hung, & Chen, 2014).

The timing of assessment

Conducting assessment activities or combining assessment and instruction does not have to be complicated. The same is true for the reshaping of the learning tasks as a result of the conclusions drawn from the assessment process. We believe that looking at the timing of the assessment in terms of whether it is carried out "in-action" or "post-action" can be a useful way for sport educators to decide on the best timing for promoting learners' self- or peer-assessment activities.

In-action assessment

Sometimes, simple solutions are quite effective as assessment activities can be manifested in more simplified ways. Assessment can be conducted during learners' practice. Box 10.7 provides an example of in-action (self-)assessment. Learners can also be assessed by their peers in action (see Box 10.8) while everyone is practicing. Sport educators can also choose to rotate learners between player and game-play analyst roles (see Chapter 5) to assess each other.

Post-action assessment

The analysis of learners' motor performance (and social development) can be achieved with reference to a more systematic and structured set of assessment indicators (see Chapter 11) and using direct (real-time observation) or indirect (video-based observation) strategies. In the latter, learners (or sports educators) can collect video footage of their task practice and engage in *post-task analysis and performance assessment*. Very often, based on videotaped footage, sport educators carry out more reliable assessments after the end of coaching sessions/PE classes (see Chapter 12 for technology tips).

Assessment and the responsive modification of learning goals and tasks

Appropriate assessment can inform the type of tasks and the necessary modifications to be applied to them, either in the next task (if the assessment is done between task transition) or in the next practice session (if the assessment is done after the session). With this interplay in mind, self- and peer-assessment can be manifested through several dynamics. Next, we provide three examples in which the processes of assessment and setting of learning goals unfold in a linked and dynamic way.

Self-regulatory (implicit) assessment. In the following example, the task structure allows the learners to assess their performance and adjust their action accordingly. The assignment contains implicit self-assessment opportunities.

Box 10.7 Task: setting the context for self-regulatory assessment

TASK GOAL: Introducing the overhand service action in volleyball.
CONTEXT: Learners are expected to struggle at the first contact with the action.
TASK CONDITIONS: Lower the net; learners may approach the net to perform the overhand service at 4–5m from the net.

TASK UNFOLDING AND LEARNER RESPONSE: Task modifications prompted too simple a task for some more evolved learners, and too difficult demands for lower-skilled learners.

INTERVENTION: Implementation of self-regulatory assessment: (i) every time the learners perform three consecutive serve errors, they take one step forward (i.e., closer to the net); (ii) every time the learners succeed in three consecutive actions, they move one step backwards (i.e., farther away from the net). This very simple rule devises a self-regulating mechanism that provides a more individualized and fine-tuned approach within the same learning task and while keeping the goals intact.

VARIANT: Most learners quickly achieve high short-term efficacy, but their skill execution is poor (low efficiency), which may later impair the accuracy and/or tactical use of the service action. Next, the learning goal is kept but the task conditions are changed. In 1v1 cooperative games, learners must perform three appropriate tosses (the ball should fall slightly in front of the learners and in the midline of the body or closer to their foot) before they perform another serve.

NOTE: This criterion will allow learners not only to self-assess the quality of their toss, but also to be aware about the importance of tossing the ball to serve in an accurate and efficient way.

Box 10.8 Task: setting the context for peer-assessment

TASK GOAL: Overhand serve; manipulate environmental conditions to refine learners' performance under pressure conditions and prompt peer-coaching and assessment interactions; the task is only completed when learners reach the endline.

TASK CONDITIONS: Learners are set in heterogenous learning teams, and the class is challenged as a whole; the new (covert) goal is to see how learners perform under pressure and their level of companionship. All learners need to perform several sets of three consecutive successful overhand serves (to gain the right to move backwards); they should not make three consecutive errors (they must move forward to approach the net again). The new (overt) goal stated to the learners is that the drill will only end when all learners are serving behind the court endline (or any other specific distance).

TASK UNFOLDING AND LEARNER RESPONSE: The most skilled learners reach the endline after some time of practice. Lower-skilled learners show inconsistent on and off plays. A new task modification is applied. Teams earn points for every learner who manages to reach the endline. Higher-skilled learners can continue to free practice the serve after reaching this goal, or alternatively, **they can assess the practice of their struggling teammates and provide peer feedback.** The points are doubled for each overhead serve performed by lower-skilled learners that was immediately preceded by feedback from a higher-skilled mate.

NOTE: Although the performance criteria are predominantly centred on the lower-skilled learners' goal achievement, their higher-skilled peers will benefit from the cognitive and social development opportunities provided by the peer-coaching interactions (see Chapter 12).

Peer-assessment for widening task goal achievement. In Box 10.8, the context is set to request peer-assessment and feedback interactions triggered by the need for manifestations of positive interdependence among learners. The task structure and instructional interactions (i.e., learners who are assigned to peer-coaching duties) are adjusted according to learners' responses.

Assessment for task goals progression. Imagine that in a short period of time, most learners in the class achieved high overhead serve success rates, although still not showing high technical quality. Even though this skill is not yet refined, the sport educator notes that the serve of most players is too demanding for most learners' current serve-reception level. The class ability to sustain game rallies becomes poor. In this case, the sport educator realizes that to continue to pursue learners' play quality, the learning goal for future classes will need to be placed on the quality of the serve-reception actions.

Self-processing questions

Box 10.9 A time to reflect – content review

- How can we better link learning and assessment?
- Why should ongoing assessments be more valued than isolated and formal assessments?
- How can you build tailor-made assessments that respect intra- and inter-individual variability in learning?

Summary and key points

This chapter acknowledged and highlighted the importance of guaranteeing the ecological validity in the ongoing linkage between teaching, learning and assessment. Considering the non-linear nature of learning, we underlined the need to develop tailor-made and flexible tools and/or assessment protocols. Framed upon a learner-oriented approach, we proposed (and exemplified) a dynamical perspective in which learning goals are ongoingly assessed and adapted according to learners' feedback. From this viewpoint, we claim that each learning activity must be seen as an opportunity for assessment, and each assessment must also be considered as a learning opportunity. Throughout this retroactive feebdback process, it is important to considerer the interplay between three dimensions of assessment (i.e., goal, task, and learners) so that the evaluation of the pedagogical intervention is not reduced exclusively to the learners' dimension.

References

Educators, S. A.-S. o. H. a. P. (2014). *National standards & grade-level outcomes for K-12 physical education*. Champaign, IL: Human Kinetics.

Entwistle, N. (2000). *Promoting deep learning through teaching and assessment: Conceptual frameworks and educational contexts*. Paper presented at the Teaching and Learning Research Programme Conference, Leicester.

Entwistle, N., & Peterson, E. (2004). Conceptions of learning and knowledge in higher education. Relationships with study behaviour and influences of learning environments. *International Journal of Educational Research, 41*, 407–428.

Espinoza, O. (2007). Solving the equity–equality conceptual dilemma: A new model for analysis of the educational process. *Educational Research, 49*(4), 343–363. doi: 10.1080/00131880701717198

Hwang, G.-J., Hung, C.-M., & Chen, N.-S. (2014). Improving learning achievements, motivations and problem-solving skills through a peer assessment-based game development approach. *Educational Technology Research and Development, 62*(2), 129–145. doi: 10.1007/s11423-013-9320-7

López-Pastor, V. M., Kirk, D., Lorente-Catalán, E., MacPhail, A., & Macdonald, D. (2013). Alternative assessment in physical education: A review of international literature. *Sport, Education and Society, 18*(1), 57–76. doi: 10.1080/13573322.2012.713860

Pinder, R. A., Davids, K., Renshaw, I., & Araújo, D. (2011). Representative learning design and functionality of research and practice in sport. *Journal of Sport & Exercise Psychology, 33*(1), 146–155. doi: 10.1123/jsep.33.1.146

van de Ruit, M., & Grey, M. J. (2019). Interindividual variability in use-dependent plasticity following visuomotor learning: The effect of handedness and muscle trained. *Journal Motor Behaviour, 51*(2), 171–184. doi: 10.1080/00222895.2018.1446125

Yell, M. L., Collins, J., Kumpiene, G., & Bateman, D. (2020). The individualized education program: Procedural and substantive requirements. *Teaching Exceptional Children, 52*(5), 304–318. doi: 10.1177/0040059920906592

Additional resources

Gardner, J. (editor) (2011). *Assessment and learning* (2nd ed.). London: SAGE Publishing.

Hay, P., & Penney, D. (2014). *Assessment in physical education. A sociocultural perspective*. Abingdon: Routledge.

Lund, J., & Veal, M. L. (2013). *Assessment-driven instruction in physical education*. Hanover, PA: Human Kinetics.

11 Implementing Learner-Oriented Assessment Strategies

Cláudio Farias, José Afonso, Ana Ramos, Patrícia Coutinho, Peter A. Hastie, Pedro Esteves, Bruno Travassos and Isabel Mesquita

---

Box 11.1 Objectives

At the end of this chapter, you will be able to:

- Adopt learner-oriented assessments strategies.
- Critically self-reflect and assess your level of development as a learner-oriented sport educator.
- Establish coherent and formative assessment of learners' development (social and motor domains).

Box 11.2 Key sections

- Introduction
- Introductory note
- How am I doing as a learner-oriented sport educator?
- Social development assessment
- Game competence assessment
- Holistic development assessment.

Introduction

This chapter proposes a multidimensional assessment of learners' development. Sport educators may assess a varied set of skills that are expected to be developed by learners, and our proposal rests on basic principles. First, the sport educators must assess what they actually teach in their classes or training sessions, or the skills for which

DOI: 10.4324/9781003140016-15

they created conditions for implicit learning to occur (through exploration activities). This can occur through peer-led and collaborative work interactions, or even as a result of the learner's investment in self-study and connection between the sporting context and the wider culture. Second, this proposal enables the sport educator to meet the intra- and inter-individual variability of learners and the strict alignment between what is taught and what is assessed. The goal is that the assessment process is essentially formative and feeds back into new learning and understanding of the subject matter of sport and games as well as social and personal development.

Although specific indicators and criteria are offered, and eventually with different weights and interpretations, these are not to be applied linearly. Nonetheless, the information regarding the assessment process must be systematized, obeying a certain organization and order. An overly dispersed and abstract representation of information will not be useful to the sport educator or the learner. It will be up to sport educators to assign meaning to the selected criteria as they experiment with the practical application of these proposals in their daily practice (Arthur & Capel, 2015).

Therefore, we offer sport educators a plan to help them self-monitor their progress as learner-oriented adepts. Tools to assess learners' social (e.g., positive leadership and social inclusion attitudes) and motor skills, as well as the holistic skill development (e.g., role-playing assessment) are also provided.

Introductory note

The assessment process in a learner-oriented approach has a strong constructive and positive tone, which highlights and values the strengths of the learners (what they can deliver with their unique motor and personal innate abilities). Points for improvement are also registered, but in a healthy context of facing and dealing with the error in a problem-solving logic. The errors and problems become indicators of possible reference aspects to encourage learners' self and collective excelling. Thus, we encourage sport educators to choose qualitative assessment indicators of motor and social performance that do not socially label learners in a negative way (William, 2011).

That said, evaluative rubrics such as 'struggling a bit', 'getting better', 'I'm there', or 'explorer', 'adventurous', and 'wizard' may be appropriate terms (embedding less value judgement) to differentiate where learners sit in their developmental journey.

Box 11.3 Key concept: a potential 'taxonomy' for formative assessment

EXPLORER: They are at the 'base of the mountain' adapting to the challenges imposed on them and exploring ways to skill development (or social competence). With a little more guidance, practice, and encouragement, the explorers will feel more confident in getting the job done.

ADVENTUROUS: They are on the 'slope of the mountain' and have a certain skill proficiency (or social competence), venturing into different activities that will allow them to reach the top of the mountain. They are on the right path but can go further.

WIZARD: They reached the 'top of the mountain'. They perform the skill proficiently and are ready to practice it in increasingly complex situations. They can explore new games and encourage less experienced climbers to believe they can too.

(Garbeloto et al. 2022) This text is part of the report of the Meu Educativo© application, which is a product of the company Educativo Tecnologia e Apoio a Educação LTDA.

How am I doing as a learner-oriented sport educator?

Given the eminently responsive character[1] and concern with responding to the individual needs of learners, sport educators must include self-critical reflective practice in their routines. This can easily be fulfilled through a *reflective diary* where sport educators map the more technical components of the teaching-learning process (characteristics of the tasks presented, learners' responses to them), but also their anxieties, struggles, critical reflections, pedagogical intentions, and their need-improvement practices.

We offer a proposal that may help the sport educators to better locate themselves on their professional development pathway as facilitators of learning. This proposal relies on self-training and the possibility of assigning different criteria to the assessment (see 'Possible self-assessment variants' below). For example, Table 11.1 allows to simultaneously map the level of responsibility attributed to learners in the different dimensions of instruction (e.g., content selection, task presentation) and it locates the scaffolding means used by the sport educators, and the predominant intervention settings and operations they use (e.g., guided practice). Sport educators can map their most predominant type of pedagogical intervention, as well as follow that trail over time. This self-analysis can be performed immediately after a session or at the end of the week. The sport educator records their perception of what has been done. They can compare this analysis with the content of their training plan or ask another sport educator to run that analysis and confront the two sheets to check for accuracy.

Sport educator self-assessment

The proposal presented in Table 11.1 holds endless possibilities. Sport educators (or, for example, a mentor, a department head) can manage the developmental intentions of the analysis as they see fit (MacPhail, Tannehill, & Goc Karp, 2013). Here we present some of these options:

Table 11.1 Scaffolding self-mapping sheet

Scaffolding self-mapping sheet															
Indicators															
Learner responsibility	Number/classification of events														
Content selection															
Task presentation															
Task monitoring (feedback)															
Task assessment															
Scaffolding means															
Demonstration															
Explanation															
Instruction															
Questioning															
Hints															
Exploratory-based															
Scaffolding setting and operations															
Pre/post briefing															
Guided practice															
In-task intervention															
Guided task structure															
Guided task presentation															
Corners' meeting															
Guided observation															
Group discussion															

- Frequency records. The taxonomy never (N), occasionally (O), or frequently (F) can offer a notion of the frequency of occurrence of each indicator.
- Leadership frequency. The 'shared between sport educator and learners' (Sh), 'sport educator-led' (SEL), or 'learner-led' (LL) taxonomy maps the frequency of the interactions and who is leading the activities.
- Type of task (context). You can easily replace the 'session number row' (and respective ticking box column) by four columns: warm-up (WU); skill task (ST); tactical task (TT); or full game (FG). You can then cross the type of task with the level of instructional responsibility transferred to learners. You might conclude that the active participation of learners in instruction does not include more complex high-order content (TT), or just the opposite, that children were progressively in charge of more complex tasks.
- Rating. Loosely, it is possible to attribute an increasing quantification to the different indicators, according to sports educators' self-perception of their ability to operationalize each process. Assigning learners with the leadership of content selection (1 point) may be less demanding than actively involving them in self- and peer-assessment activities (4 points). The same premise applies to scaffolding indicators. Guided practice may be deemed less instructionally demanding than applying guided observation scaffolding. They can be scored with different weights.
- Process mastery. If sport educators find the rating 'scrutiny' difficult to manage, they may opt for a more self-referenced assessment. Sport educators' perception of their ability to efficiently apply each strategy can be ascertained using indicators such as 'struggling a bit' (S), 'getting better' (GB), 'I'm there' (IT). If sport educators can manage emotionally their self-assessment in a positive way, a quantitative score and setting of coaching/teaching goals may be appropriate (e.g., S = 1 point, GB = 2 points, on IT =3 points).

Social development assessment

A learner-oriented assessment aspires heavily to inclusion promotion. Therefore, high importance is assigned to the development of various social skills that can implicitly contribute to this goal (see team charting scores). This section presents several possibilities that sport educators might find appealing and easy to handle.

Equity and inclusion assessment

The level of inclusion or equity of participation in activities can be measured quantitatively. Sport educators (or learners) may (i) measure the participation time of each learner in game-play activities (see Table 11.2) or/and (ii) quantify learners' actual on-the-ball participation (see Table 11.3).[2]

Box 11.4 Key point: assessing equity and inclusion

Equity and inclusion assessment is important in that learners can self-assess their perception of participation in activities, and later confront it with objective data about that participation. The inferences drawn from these data can be discussed at sport panels (or social-focused group discussions) (Chapter 5).

Descriptive narratives

The sport educator can also make descriptive narratives of learners' participation in games or scaffold the narrative analysis of the analysts or team captains. It will be helpful to have some indicators of how inclusive/segregating attitudes may manifest during game-based activities (Farias, 2017). For example, these behaviours can be expressed in the simple act of a player not passing the ball to a certain teammate, in the form of unpleasant and discriminatory verbal interactions, or

Table 11.2 Participation time of each learner in game-play activities

Game: Netball (4v4)

Lesson/camera/ video n°:				*Match total time:*				
	Playing time							
Player:	in	out	Sub total	in	out	Sub total	in	out	total

Note: In each team, learners take turns in the analyst role using a stopwatch.

Table 11.3 Learners' on-the-ball participation

Game: Lacrosse (5v3 + goalkeeper)

Match n°: _____   Match total time: _____

Player:	Throw S	Throw N	Catch Y	Catch N	Dribble Y	Dribble N	Shot Y	Shot N	Total

Note: A X is placed in each box per each player's on-the-ball actions. The participation rate represents the sum of successful and unsuccessful actions. A percentage of success can also be calculated (total success plays/total success + unsuccess plays). Importantly, you can add an off-the-ball indicator (e.g., available but not passed/or targeted) to value players' effort in support moves. Total rate of play can also be calculated (total participation actions/total time played).

they can occur when certain circumstances are combined (in the moments immediately following a defeat, when certain practitioners are grouped in the same teams, etc.).

Social responsibility

A learner-oriented approach also requires learners to exhibit high levels of personal and social responsibility. These include taking responsibility for their roles(s) in the design and presentation of games or showing acceptance of peers on an individual and team level (Lund & Shanklin, 2011). The most common format of providing students with feedback is using rating scales and checklists. Table 11.4 provides a sample checklist that can be used to provide learners with some source of feedback about their social development progress. Several discrete positive social attitudes may be assessed.[3]

Leadership assessment

Positive peer-leadership on the part of peer-coaches involves the active building of relationships with peers based on personal, emotional, and inspirational exchanges with the goal of helping to develop each team member to their fullest potential (see Chapter 5). The assessment of leadership skills can be carried out in a self-assessment format aimed

Table 11.4 Assessment of discrete positive social attitudes

	Scoring		
Desired behavior	*Emerging (1)*	*Approaching (2)*	*Target (3)*
Seeks opportunities to learn			
Practices hard			
Accepts advice			
Participates enthusiastically			
Shows responsibility			
Cooperates with others			
Shows tolerance to others			
Commits to the team			
Plays fairly			

at the peer-coaches' critical reflection on their performance and the nature of the interactions they build with others.

Any simplified reflexive prompts can have a significant effect on changing negative attitudes. This can include taking self-critical notes in a *'role-playing journal'* regarding questions like "how do I feel in my role?", "am I doing everything in my power to help all my mates?", "what am I already doing very well and what do I need to improve in my leadership?".

Some leadership frameworks have been adapted to the context of peer-coaching interactions to better understand learners' leadership potential to contribute to positive social interactions (e.g., Callow, Smith, Hardy, Arthur, & Hardy, 2009). The assessment example given in Table 11.5 compiles some of the leadership skills (both instructional and social management) that may be realistically developed in young people. These skills can be listed in increasing degrees of demand. The teams might choose to assess their peer-leaders providing independent and confidential feedback on their leaders' needs-improvement issues.

Table 11.5 Leadership skills assessment

Peer leadership assessment sheet

		Score
Wizard	Promotes knowledge exchanges between teammates	3
	Shares decision-making with teammates	3
	Recognises that different teammates have different needs and personalities	3
	Leads responsible peer-questioning	3
Adventurous	Helps teammates to solve their problems	2
	Encourages teammates to be team players	2
	Leads by example not just by telling	2
	Leads responsible feedback to teammates	2
Explorer	Is critical of inequity and discriminatory attitudes	1
	Knows the strengths and weakness of each teammate	1
	Talks optimistically	1
	Leads responsible task presentation	1

Game competence assessment

Tailoring what is assessed to what is taught and to learners' developmental stage

Even if high relevance is attributed to learners' development of social and collaborative skills, learners are still learning to play games. Thus, overlooking the value of learners' achievement of motor goals may result in overlooking the authenticity of the sporting experience they are living. In this sense, it is important to also involve learners in taking records related to sports performance.[4] The sport educator may choose to limit the recording of information to one or another key learning task in the practice session.

Box 11.5 Key point: assessment and intra- and inter-individual variability

To attend to intra- and inter-individual variability, the sport educator can choose to differentiate and narrow the appreciation of the game components according to what was most trained by each learner or based on their most notable strengths. Students may also be asked to indicate on which indicators they prefer to be assessed.

In this process, it is important that specific motor skills are brought to the forefront, as well as the level of alignment between the specific task goals and learners' responses (see Box 11.6 and Table 11.6).

Box 11.6 Task: setting individualized assessment criteria

SETTING: Field hockey 4v3 plus 2 floaters game form.

ASSESSMENT CRITERIA: Lower-skilled learners (Explorers) – use basic grip to hold the implement; change speed after passing; higher-skilled learners (Adventurous) – attack quickly with a pass to the side-lines, followed by a quick cut towards the goal.

NOTE: During the game many different situations will occur, but in this task learners only score points for each time they fulfil the task criteria.

Table 11.6 Game-play observation sheet

Game-play observation sheet		
Analyst:	*Analyst team:*	*Analyst score*:*
Task: Field hockey 4v3 plus 2 floaters	*Criteria – adventurous: attacks quickly with a pass to the side-lines, followed by a quick cut towards the goal; used body feint in one-on-one plays*	*Criteria – explorer: uses basic grip to hold the implement (v grip); changes speed after passing*
Teams	Events	
A Explorers Adventurous		
B Explorer Adventurous		

Note: *Analyst self-assessment based on 'struggling a bit' (S), 'getting better (GB), 'I'm there', (IT). You can also self-assign a quantitative score for yourself (e.g., S = 1, GB = 2, on IT = 3).

Assessing decision-making and skill performance ability

The next example aligns with the practical proposal for teaching futsal through appropriateness-based manipulation of task constraints (see Chapter 7).[5]

Following the principles for the design of learning activities, and the exemplary tasks that have been previously offered, the assessment of learning should consider the individual sensitivity of learners to pick up information from the environment (i.e., *attunement*) to fulfil the task goals. With that purpose, sport educators could consider the use of the Game Performance Evaluation Tool (GPET), which has proven to be reliable in assessing problem-solving skills (Pizarro, Práxedes, Travassos, Villar, & Moreno, 2019). This tool focuses on learners' tactical development by considering decision-making and execution within the game environment. The assessment involves the evaluation of the decision and the action of learners by assigning the value 1 to appropriate decisions/executions and 0 to inappropriate decisions/executions. For instance, in handball, learners could be assessed while performing key game-skills such as passing, dribbling, and shooting, in relation to different principles of play: keeping ball possession, progress towards the goal, and shot at the goal. The output of this assessment will inform the sport educator on the percentage of successful decisions and executions of the learners on each game-skill.

The assessment of learning could also entail a behavioural focus, the monitoring of the congruence between the expected tactical actions of each learning phase, and the occurrence of those tactics within specific small-sided games. For instance, in basketball, a 3v3 game could be implemented to ascertain if the intended game-play actions take place according to the specific manipulation of constraints. In this 3v3 small-sided game, the larger the court size the better spatial occupation by learners (i.e., a triangular disposition of the team on the court). Sport educators could access the frequency of occurrence and the respective quality of players' execution according to the specific manipulation of constraints. Using the same exemplary task, the assessment of an effective exploration of a 1v1 or, in alternative, the exploration of a combination of movements (i.e., passing to a teammate) could also be accomplished in view of the expected behaviour (i.e., pertinency) and the correspondent constraint manipulation. In this case, the lesser number of defenders involved should amplify the opportunities for the off-the-ball attackers to receive a pass and shoot at the basket (i.e., expected behaviour).

Holistic development assessment

Role-playing assessment

Role-playing assessment evaluates the performance of the same function (a sport-based role) but it is individually tailored to the strengths of the learners. The sport educator must take particular care in assigning different roles to different learners and hold students accountable accordingly. Therefore, the more or less formal assessment of role-playing should come as complement and not as a burden. For instance, the selection of peer-coaches for the job must ensure that these students have the minimum conditions to perform that role (i.e., a knowledge level superior to peers to provide asymmetrical knowledge exchange in a socially rewarding way). Assigning this role to students with poor organizational skills can become an unpleasant experience for them as the chances of having success in this task will be slim. A learner with exceptional digital skills can become a digital technology manager and a born public relations manager can be appointed as a sport director. As students become more and more familiar with role-playing and develop more trust and stronger social ties with peers, they may self-propose to try out other roles.

The process of assessing role-playing will be facilitated if sport educators deliver a series of descriptors and operational expectations that they want to see in the performance of each role. These responsibilities can be ranked by level of complexity to which different scoring weights are assigned[6] (e.g., for digital technology managers supervising their team's website will be more demanding than simply sending information by email to colleagues). As they feel more confident, or according to their availability, learners can self-propose to perform roles holding different demands. The accomplishment of tasks with different complexity (which requires further investment and effort from learners) are also scored differently.

Table 11.7 exemplifies a record sheet of the referee's role, applicable both in competitive events held within the team or between teams of

Table 11.7 Refereeing scoring sheet

Refereeing scoring sheet				
Referees	Referees' team	yes (3 points)	Not always but they tried (2 point)	No but they were friendly (1 point)
John and Liza	Blue bibs			
Were the referees fair to both teams?				
Do the referees know the rules of the game and the signs?				
Did the referees maintain a calm and moderate attitude throughout the event?				
Total scoring				

different institutions, and in any training session that the sport educator feels appropriate to consider it.

Peer-assessment can be used as the peer-coaches in that play session or any other group of learners (this can be a task for the sport panel, Chapter 5) can fill in the refereeing scoring sheet at the end of the match. This principle can extend to any other role-playing scoring (analyst, inclusion captain, sport director).

Assessment in learner-designed games

Offering the opportunity to design their own games offers learners a unique setting to practice specific sport skills, but also to develop a more sophisticated understanding of game structures and game-play. They achieve this through actively engaging with components of game-play and thinking critically about their sport learning experiences (Hastie, 2010). For that, they need to have certain dispositions and exhibit specific behaviours to create 'good games'. In learner-designed games, we hope students have positive attitudes towards working co-operatively and solving problems in groups. These may include the search for learning opportunities, participate enthusiastically, as well as accept and act on advice.

Figure 11.1 uses the technique known as a 'semantic differential' in which the players indicate their stance on a scale between two bipolar adjective pairs (e.g., boring and exciting). Players simply place a check mark in the appropriate box. Those on the far left are considered the least desirable, and score 1, while those on the right are the more desired and score 7.

Boring	|...|...|...|...|...|...|...|	Exciting
Low Activity	|...|...|...|...|...|...|...|	High Activity
No challenge	|...|...|...|...|...|...|...|	Highly Challenging
Too Complicated	|...|...|...|...|...|...|...|	Easy to Understand
Bad Player Number	|...|...|...|...|...|...|...|	Playing Number Right
No Skill Developed	|...|...|...|...|...|...|...|	Develops Skills Well
Complicated scoring	|...|...|...|...|...|...|...|	Good Scoring System
Wrong Playing Area	|...|...|...|...|...|...|...|	Good Playing Area
Wrong Equipment	|...|...|...|...|...|...|...|	Good Equipment
Poor Safety	|...|...|...|...|...|...|...|	Safety Addressed

Figure 11.1 Game evaluation scoresheet.

Some direction should be given to learners: 'Place a mark in the space that describes your feelings about the game you have just played'. The spaces in the middle represent a neutral opinion, while those closer to the edges represent a stronger opinion either way.

Team chart scoring

It is up to sport educators to choose which learning outcomes to highlight; performance-oriented: 'how many times did you get to base?'; personal and social development-oriented: 'from 1 to five how would you score their praising of their teammates'; or process-oriented: 'how many times did they feint and fast-break before supporting?'. As a team, learners can use this information to define goal-oriented

Table 11.8 Team chart scoring

Sport: Softball					
Team name:	*Session*				
	1	*2*	*3*	*4*	*...*
Social scores (1 to 5)					
Responsibility					
Effort and commitment					
Equity in game-play participation					
Inclusive and peer support attitudes					
Game-play scores (frequency, successful trials)					
Getting on base					
Moving the runner					
Defending space by infield, outfield position					
Task criteria scores					
Role-playing scores (1 to 5)					
Learner (name) Role					
Josh coach					
Lia referee					
Session scoring					
Total scoring					

activities (game tasks), their teams' competition strategy, or even set an action plan to change less appropriate social attitudes, for example, during the sport panel discussions (Farias, Mesquita, Hastie, & O'Donovan, 2018). Table 11.8 provides a team chart example. The sport educator should note the balance between the social (5 items) and performance scorings (5 items) and consequent holistic recognition of learner merit and achievement.

Self-processing questions

Box 11.7 A time to reflect – content review

- Describe five potential indicators to ascertain your current and ongoing scaffolding practice.
- Build a team scoring chart for your next teaching unit (or coaching micro-cycle) including one criterion from each assessment dimension (social development, competence, etc.).
- Choose one learning task and state how you are going to adjust your assessment according to intra- and inter-individual variability.

Summary and key points

This chapter offers a proposal for a multidimensional assessment of learners' development considering their participation in learner-oriented pedagogies. The proposal considers a plan for the sport educator to be able to self-monitor their progress as a learner-oriented adept, to assess learners' social and motor skills, as well as the holistic development of their capabilities. We highlight that sport educators should include self-critical reflective practice in their routines to map the more technical components of the teaching-learning process, but also to locate them in their individual professional development pathway. We provide examples of social development assessment tools, such as equity and inclusion and leadership assessment. Examples of game competence assessment related to motor performance outcomes are also offered. Finally, we underline the importance of considering the holistic development of learners based on the assessment of role-playing and learner-designed games.

Notes

1 See the Chapters on scaffolding to picture the dynamic nature of sport educators' instruction (e.g., contingency).
2 You can find out more about this topic in Gréhaigne, Godbout, and Bouthier (1997)'s proposal of the Team Sport Assessment Procedure and in the Mitchell, Oslin, and Griffin (2020)'s Game Performance Assessment Instrument.
3 In turn, the sport educator can make clusters of several discrete positive social attitudes that sum up into the team chart under one of the main indicators selected (e.g., 'Effort and commitment').
4 It is important that learners occasionally have the possibility to analyze their own motor performance using video records of that performance (e.g., through iPads). During their habitual practice, learners are mostly dependent on external analysis (from peers or the coach educator) as they are unable to analyze themselves in all angles and components of their motor practice.
5 This might be an appropriate proposal in older youth sport or secondary physical education contexts. A more formalized and performance-oriented stance is followed.
6 See above 'Leadership assessment'.

References

Arthur, J., & Capel, S. (2015). How planning and evaluation support effective learning and teaching. In S. Capel & M. Whitehead (Eds.), *Learning to teach physical education in the secondary school: A companion to school experience (4th edition)* (pp. 31–48). Abingdon, OX: Routledge.

Callow, N., Smith, M. J., Hardy, L., Arthur, C. A., & Hardy, J. (2009). Measurement of transformational leadership and its relationship with team cohesion and performance level. *Journal of Applied Sport Psychology, 21*(4), 395–412.

Farias, C. (2017). Promoting equity and social responsibility in sport education. *Active+ Healthy Journal (ACHPER), 24*(2), 35–42.

Farias, C., Mesquita, I., Hastie, P. A., & O'Donovan, T. (2018). Mediating peer teaching for learning games: An action research intervention across three consecutive sport education seasons. *Research Quarterly for Exercise and Sport, 89*(1), 91–102.

Garbeloto, F., Santos, R., Garganta, R., Maia, J. (2022). Meu Educativo: A new technological tool to assess and monitor physical and motor competence. In *Studies in Child Motor Development XV* (v.1, p. 73). Higher School of Education and Communication University of Algarve.

Gréhaigne, J. F., Godbout, P., & Bouthier, D. (1997). Performance assessment in team sports. *Journal of Teaching in Physical Education, 16*(4), 500–516.

Hastie, P. (2010). *Student-designed games: Strategies for promoting creativity, cooperation, and skill development.* Champaign: Human Kinetics.

Lund, J., & Shanklin, J. (2011). The impact of accountability on student performance in a secondary physical education badminton unit. *Physical Educator, 68*(4), 210–220.

MacPhail, A., Tannehill, D., & Goc Karp, G. (2013). Preparing physical education preservice teachers to design instructionally aligned lessons through constructivist pedagogical practices. *Teaching and Teacher Education, 33,* 100–112.

Mitchell, S. A., Oslin, J., & Griffin, L. L. (2020). *Teaching sport concepts and skills: A tactical games approach.* Champaign: Human Kinetics.

Pizarro, D., Práxedes, A., Travassos, B., Villar, F., & Moreno, A. (2019). The effects of a nonlinear pedagogy training program in the technical-tactical behaviour of youth futsal players. *International Journal of Sports Science & Coaching, 14*(1), 15–23.

Wiliam, D. (2011). What is assessment for learning? *Studies in Educational Evaluation, 37*(1), 3–14.

Additional Resource

Hay, P., & Penney, D. (2012). *Assessment in physical education: A sociocultural perspective.* Oxford, UK: Routledge.

12 Empowering Learners' Self-Assessment, Peer-Assessment, and Sport Learning Through Technology

José Afonso, Cláudio Farias, Ana Ramos, Cristiana Bessa, Patrícia Coutinho and Isabel Mesquita

---

Box 12.1 Objectives

At the end of this chapter, you will be able to:

- Understand how technology can help learners' self- and peer-assessment.
- Scaffold learners' progressive active engagement in technology-based self- and peer-assessment activities.

Box 12.2 Key sections

- Introduction.
- Why is learner-led assessment important, what does technology add, and what precautions should we take?
- Technology tools in Physical Education and youth sport.
- Scaffolding learners' use of technology for self- and peer-assessment.
- A practical application of technology-based, self- and peer-assessment activities.

Introduction

Self- and peer-assessment are key pedagogical fundaments of a learner-oriented approach to teaching and learning sport and games in Physical Education (PE) and youth sport contexts. This aligns sondly with the active engagement of learners in the collaborative

DOI: 10.4324/9781003140016-16

problem-solving framework advocated throughout this book and their consequent participation in cycles of observation, identification, and assessment that inform subsequent devising of action plans. As an additional sophistication step, this chapter offers sport educators a possibility of using technologies to implement learner-oriented assessment activities. Likely, this establishes the ultimate bridge between the sporting experiences lived by learners and their daily social and cultural world where technologies are a pervasive part of their daily lives. Although many technologies are currently being applied at high-level sports, this chapter will focus on solutions that may more easily be implemented in PE and youth sport contexts, with reduced financial investment.

The use of self- and peer-assessment tools in a sport learning context is a challenging process. Real-life scenarios are subjective to a point that learners may find it difficult to focus attention on the most relevant components of the task goal achievement that informs their self- and peer-assessment. Even when learners are successful in observing, identifying, and diagnosing their needs-improvement game-play attributes (e.g., poor passing skills, poor closing space as a team), cause and effect relationships are multiple and varied, and the assessment of game-play action may become a dauting task for inexperienced learners.

However, if properly scaffolded by sport educators, technology might assist with improving these processes, adding that 'extra' motivational ingredient to the experience, becoming a powerful means of development of game-play and social skills (Moore & Fry, 2017).

Box 12.3 Key point: collecting video images of learners' practice

Typical learner-led assessment activities can be applied through real time, on-the-spot direct observation methods during the natural course of any youth sport or PE training session. However, in a learners' self- and peer-assessment approach based on technology use, the unfolding of pedagogical activities implies that the sport educator (or the learners themselves) collects video images of learners' sport practice. This will form the baseline upon which learners can develop their observation and diagnosis skills (identification of problems in the practice), subsequent planning (content and task selection or task design), and implementation of action plans to resolve their game-play weaknesses.

This chapter showcases how sport educators can scaffold learners' use of technology to promote productive learner-led assessment processes. Importantly, in following the appropriateness-based thread of this book, this proposal attempts to promote a coherent alignment between learners, learning goals, and tasks. A progressive and scaffolded practical proposal on the implementation of technology-based learner-oriented assessment activities is offered.

Why is learner-oriented assessment important, what does technology add, and what possible precautions should we take?

At the outset, it is important to clarify the main evidence-based benefits of the involvement of learners in the high-order cognitive processes associated with learner-oriented assessment activities and the use of technology. We also point out some precautions in the use of technology (Harris & Brown, 2018).

Benefits of reflective observation and self- and peer-assessment:
- Promotion of high cognitive engagement in learning and deeper understanding of sport and games, developing a greater sense of autonomy, self-awareness, and self-esteem.
- Finding explanatory reasons for errors and problems facilitate the relationship between cognition (mental analysis) and action (motor solution) and increase the learners' ability to monitor their own practice and modify it autonomously.
- Learners develop a sense of greater control over their own sport development, as they can better understand the efficiency factors (processes: e.g., skill execution) that may influence their efficacy (outcomes: e.g., scoring a goal).
- The focus on positive self- and peer-assessment perceives the limitations and strengths of every learner as an elemental part of practicing and learning sport and games.
- Analysis and assessment of video images of critical situations occurring during moments of competition establish a clearer relationship between the problems identified during high-demand practice (formal competition) and the definition of goals, learning content, and tasks in the sport coaching context.
- It enhances the development of social and relational skills and learners' ability to communicate, a sense of belonging, ability to cooperate, mutual help, and mutual respect.

- From a neurophysiological perspective, learners' engagement with higher-order, cognitively demanding tasks reflects greater efficiency of neuronal activation and/or communication within the brain and its functional and structural plasticity responses.

The use of technology for teaching, assessing, and learning sport and games

As a pedagogical complement, technology is a form of augmented feedback because it allows the learner to self-observe, or to observe others, gathering important information about what may be interfering with their body schema or tactical actions (Potdevin et al., 2018). There are several educational benefits in the use of technology and peer- and self-assessment:

- Immediate video-based feedback refines the assertiveness of performance analysis; learners' observation of the action increases their identification and understanding of errors and game problems.
- Most technology is user-friendly and can be used in versatile ways.
- It expedites learning by providing learners with opportunities to create pedagogical resources (e.g., worksheets and video resources available on a tablet) that they can match against task goals or a performance model and follow throughout the lesson without adult guidance.
- Some tools (video clips) allow revisiting critical moments in learners' game-play practice, through slow-down, pause or rewind analysis and fosters brainstorming about 'current practice/level' and 'desired practice/level'.
- Delayed (post-practice) feedback may provide more time for developing more reliable self- and peer-assessment.

Potential limitations of technology use

Like any pedagogical tool, the use of technology has its limitations, of which sport educators should be aware:

- The over-reliance on technology-based augmented feedback may turn learners overly dependent on external sources of information, with a potential increase in feelings of insecurity in their absence.

- The regular use of technology implies refining the lesson/training plan to maximize effective practice time and the time needed to train learners for using these tools.
- The strong participatory and collaborative component of technology-based self- and peer-assessment activities may require careful scaffolding of the quality of social interactions between learners.
- A non-mediated integration of some technology (e.g., smartphones) in PE classes or youth sport and learners' eventual lack of understanding of its educational value may lead to deviant behaviours and be a focus of distraction (e.g., social network apps are also available).

Technological tools in physical education and youth sport

A wide set of technological tools are currently used by sport educators across the globe. Casey, Goodyear, and Armour (2017) offered a remarkable collection of pedagogical cases for the enhancement of children's learning in PE using technologies. Table 12.1 revisits some of the main technologies highlighted by Casey et al. (2017) and adds a few more options to facilitate self- and peer-assessment activities in PE and youth sport.

Scaffolding learners' use of technology for self- and peer-assessment

The participation of learners in self- and peer-assessment processes through technology, although intrinsically fun, must be scaffolded by sport educators (Koekoek & van Hilvoorde, 2019). Otherwise, assessment activities may slip towards an end in themselves, without a clear connection with the sport content and task goals that best fit the specific learning needs of learners at that moment.

At a basic level of scaffolding, there are typical processes that must be mediated by sport educators. These include the everyday support provided to learners during their gradual contact with technology: (i) a progression in how each technology is used, namely expanding its practical application, correlating diverse variables, and increasing the complexity of data interpretation (e.g., progressing from the analysis and assessment of simpler individual technical skills to problems related to more complex group tactical principles); and (ii) setting a progression in learners' use of increasingly more sophisticated technologies (using YouTube video observation is far less demanding than using video clip editing software).

Table 12.1 Technology tools in physical education and youth sport

Technology/app	Functions	How can these tools be used
Laptop (device)	A laptop or tablet that can be used to access a range of apps, and that includes a camera and video function.	By learners to support engagement with multiple apps to support self- and peer- observation and diagnosis, assessment, and learning.
Portable cameras	A compact mean to capture photos and videos in highly dynamic and action settings.	Placed in a fixed place and collect images of a practice setting (e.g., game-play events) to capture collective team interactions or used by an individual learner (on a head strap) to enable the analysis, for example, of the collected information by that learner (e.g., attentional focus: decentres eyes from the ball, centres on teammates positioning or space gaps).
YouTube or similar web platforms	Video-sharing websites that allow users to upload, view, and share videos.	Sport educators show videos of expert performers as a way of introducing a task and/or sport content to learners or to scaffold peer-coaching activities.
GPS tracking systems	Provides learner tracking and delivers play participation monitoring data in real-time, it detects accelerations, decelerations, changes of direction and integrates add-on data such as heart rate (transmitted on the fly).	In outdoor high-performance youth sport teams can be used to map the range of field coverage and individual and collective intervention of learners (e.g., tactical systems and behaviour) and/or capture indicators of the type of physiological work performed (anaerobic, aerobic, high-intensity, etc.), indicates the suitability of the tasks to reaching target heart rate zone.
Heart rate monitoring	Essentially a fitness tracker. Includes built-in heart rate monitors, touchscreen, smartphone notifications, activity and health-adjacent information tracking, automatic exercise detection, and it can be couple to mobile phone devices for GPS tracking.	Learners create individual heart rate charts on station work and compare this data with recommendations on appropriate levels of physical activity.
Central nervous and cardiac systems monitoring	Provides quick-fire detailed biological data on the Central Nervous System and Cardiac System.	Suggest the sport educator how to adjust the contents and intensity of the session to suit the learner's state of readiness.

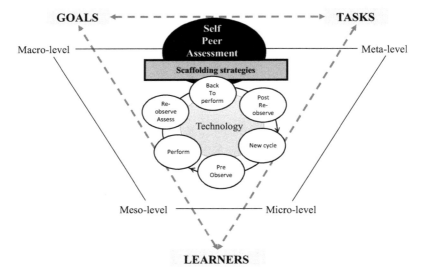

Figure 12.1 A technology-based proposal for self- and peer-assessment.

On the one hand, as represented in Figure 12.1, sport educators need to integrate the reflexive cycle inherent to the assessment process (Observe > Perform > Re-observe > Re-perform > plan >...) into content development (e.g., task progression). This involves the dynamic scaffolding of the active involvement of learners in these experiences. In other words, observation, assessment, planning, and application of new solutions or learning tasks need to be properly aligned.

Scaffolding the alignment between observation, assessment, planning, and application

We need to stress that self- and peer-assessment are an integral part of the learner-oriented teaching and learning of sport and games, and thus, they have a strong problem-solving focus (Pol, Volman, & Beishuizen, 2010). Learners should be guided to assess game performance problems (tactical or skill-based problems) related to the main barriers to their learning (game-play development). In this way, the information collected through assessment can inform more accurately what learners specifically need to work on to improve their skills (e.g., in the next task or lesson; Magdalinski, 2008). Figure 12.1 provides a potential technology-based conceptual proposal for self- and peer-assessment.

Sport educators need to align the logic of sport content development (e.g., task progression), the progressive active participation of learners in instructional processes (e.g., goal-setting, task design), and the self- and peer-assessment activities (see Figure 12.2). We now present a series of procedures related to the observation and assessment of game-play activities that sport educators should consider in preparing learners for an active participation in assessment activities.

Sparkes and Smith (2014, p. 100) defined observation as 'the rigorous act of perceiving the workings of people, culture and society through one's senses and then documenting these in field notes or recording them through technological means'. In the context of teaching and learning sport and games, the process of observation is critical to the analysis of learners' game-play development. Such a systematic observation requires the use of indirect observation methods (e.g., videotaped images), which should consider several operational principles:

- Indirect observation can be carried immediately before or after the PE lesson or practice session, or immediately after the performance of actions (e.g., after a game-based task that was selected for learners' self- or peer-assessment).
- It allows for a thorough and complete analysis of sport performance components that cannot be measured through snapshot direct observation.
- The use of technology in indirect observation is particularly useful to record behaviours of high frequency and duration where its occurrence does not allow the observer to make effective recordings and assessment in real-time.
- The use of technology in indirect observations provides an opportunity to involve multiple (to cross opinions) and individual observers[1] and the use of video clips which, with its frame-by-frame forward/backward, pause, and slow-motion functions, increases the analytic power of the observation.

In the preparation of learners for an effective observation of their own practice, their teammates' practice, or the practice of learners at other teams or institutions, sport educators should:

- Steer learners' attention to critical game-play moments and motor action components (e.g., what happens when your team and/or the opponent is defending? what happens to attackers when the ball enters on the right-side lane?).
- Steer learners' attention to important aspects of the task and/or critical components of actions, identifying those that need to be

reinforced in re-instruction and/or feedback (e.g., helping learners separate relevant information from 'noise')[2] or by scaffolding learners' changing of the task themselves to better the practice of those skills; learners will realize that not all the relevant information can be addressed at once, and so choices and priorities must be established.

– Help learners relate rationally (i.e., by analysing, reflecting, and studying the situation) and systematically (i.e., gathering objective and credible information) the causes and effects of learners' errors (e.g., the volleyball spike is being blocked because the attacker does not look at the blockers' position before spiking).

Sport educators can use a set of additional scaffolding strategies to facilitate learners' self- and peer-assessment activities (Xun & Land, 2004):

– Promote the alignment between task conditions and the assessed game-play actions. The game-based learning tasks must, in fact, enable the emergence of those motor actions (tactical content) that one wishes to assess and subsequently improve based on that assessment (see Box 12.4 below).

– Design (or help learners design) tasks and task progressions that provide learners with sufficient time for practicing their assessment skills before more formal assessment moments.

– Set a framework of problems (and assessment foci) of gradual complexity and guide learners' observation of relevant information. They may begin with the identification of simplified motor components ('check the position of their elbow') and progress to more complex tactical principles ('record how they're covering space when defending').

– During video analysis, the sport educator can teach learners how to use of diagrams and annotations in the video clips. The peer-coaches can be asked to replicate that activity next time they are introducing a task to their peers or discussing the most pressing game problems of their teams.

Box 12.4 Task: 5v5 – assessment target is the 'pass-and-cut' action (Handball); the task constraints and the assessment target should be aligned

As a prerequisite of placing learners to perform self- and peer-assessment, sport educators need to guarantee that the tasks and settings they design will afford the conditions for the emergence of the game-play actions they wish to assess. In the case of the pass-and-cut actions, the 5v5 task must provide enough space to players for performing pass-and-cut moves as an appropriate way to solve the attack problems. Therefore, the task conditions should not allow players in defence to form a fixed defensive line along the 6-metre goal area line waiting for the attack plays. If that happens, the attackers will no longer have space to perform the pass-and-cut on the back of the defenders. Thus, the assessment of the pass-and-cut will no longer be possible as the task constraints prevent the target game actions to emerge. In this case, the task would need to include conditions such as all court, man-to-man defence so that players get open space on defenders' back to perform pass-and-cut moves to attack the goal.

A practical application of technology-based, self-assessment, and peer-assessment activities

In Figure 12.2 we present an example of how sport educators can progressively integrate the self- and peer-assessment activities into the pacing of increasingly involving learners in instructional decision-making. This example is set in line with the creativity progression presented in Chapter 8.

In the schematic representation of Figure 12.2, learners are continually scaffolded along their active participation in self- and peer-assessment interactions using different technology. Below we present two practical tasks, situated at the micro- and meso-level of creativity. Based on this framework, sport educators can easily build a sequence tailored to their specific practice context that extends learners' active engagement in macro- and meta-levels of creativity or any other level of instructional and social interactions they wish.

Practice task A: micro-level

Pre-session: briefing/observe

The sport educator has previously selected a series of 1v1 game badminton sequences associated with game starts through long service: Long-serve> clear shot > lob or drop shot defence. Then, the sport educator demonstrates/repeats to learners the critical game-play components (hands and arms position and angle, grip, foot work). Each peer-coach takes his team to a practice court and implements the task.

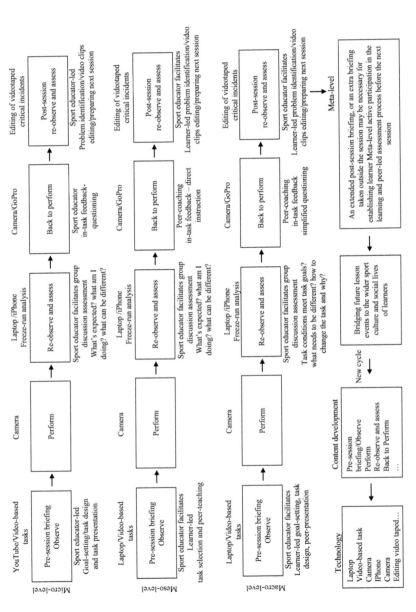

Figure 12.2 Integration of the reflexive teaching-assessment-learning cycle into content development.

Perform

Groups of 4 learners: 2 players (in) plus 1 coach-referee (off), plus 1 'filmmaker' (off).

2 players perform 1v1 (10-min). Then swap roles for another 10-min.

Re-observe and assess

The 2 filmmakers share the videotaped games with all teammates. Each learner uses their smartphones to observe, analyse, and score their individual overall game performance in a records sheet (e.g., 'top game'; 'needs some work'; 'needs serious work').

The sport educator steps in to facilitate group discussion (what's expected? what are you doing? do you agree with your mate's self-assessment? why? what needs to change?).

Back to perform

The original task is resumed. During practice, the sport educator steps in to engage learners in both convergent (lower-skilled learners: meet the pre-set criteria) and divergent (higher-skilled learners: find new solutions) tactical questioning.

Post-session re-observe and assess

The sport educator analyses the videos of all learners to identify the most pressing game problems (i.e., misalignment between current task goals and learners' game actions). The sport educator edits the videos clips of these critical incidents and sends back the videos to each learner individually. They also send them e-mail with potential practice tasks to work on the needs-improvement bits that learners should study before the next session. Peer-coaches are tasked to pre-select potential tasks to work on the next session (i.e., engaging at a meso-level of creativity).

Practice task B: meso-level

Pre-session briefing/observe

At the end of the previous session, while at home, learners were individually tasked to use their smartphones to register their perceptions of effort, tiredness, soreness, and number of hours and quality of sleep.

At the start of the next day's session, the sport educator actively engages the peer-coaches in the discussion of their own data and the data relating to their team members. While peer-coaches are briefed, the other learners assess their own current state of cardiac and neural readiness. Considering these data, the sport educator facilitates group discussion among peer-coaches on the best fitness plan to apply in the current session (e.g., higher focus on speed endurance, leg, and abdominal strength, etc.). For example, if six learners have slept three hours less than usual, they could need to engage in lower-intensity efforts and/or lower demanding tasks from a cognitive standpoint.

Perform

Learners put the work plan into practice using baton heart rate monitors.

Re-observe and assess

After the first work round, each learner analyses their individual data. The teams then discuss and take records on the extent to which their physical indicators align with the task fitness goals. The sport educator facilitates discussion within teams about potential changes to the tasks.

Back to perform

The original task is resumed. During practice, the sport educator momentarily engages peer-coaches in guided observation (see Chapter 3) to spot technical errors or lack of effort of some learners and are encourages them to step in to provide technical and motivational feedback to teammates. At this point, the peer-coaches, or any other learner taking on analyst responsibilities may use a more structured record sheet to evaluate more formally their peers' attitudes related, for example, with individual effort, collaborative group work or peer-praising attitudes (Chapter 11).

Post-session: re-observe and assess

The sport educator briefs all learners on how to correlate data from different variables (hours of sleep, physical and cognitive readiness) and assigns them a homework task. Each learner must review the feedback derived from the data and bring an individual work plan proposal to the next session (e.g., perhaps one learner is overly tired and should rest for one extra day; perhaps another learner is starting to fall below its usual values, and an alert is provided). This may also provide a need-improvement indication related with learners' social interactions ('we need to provide more motivational support to Jane or Jack').

Self-processing questions

> ### Box 12.5 A time to reflect – content review
>
> * How can you use two possible applications of laptops or tablets in PE or youth sport settings to promote self- or peer-assessment activities?
> * Based on 'Practical Task A', select a sporting content of your convenience, and design a practice session or PE lesson that expresses some of the processes presented there.

Summary and key points

This chapter shows how sport educators can scaffold the learners' use of technology to promote successful learner-oriented assessment. This proposal sets an alignment between learners, learning goals, and tasks, in which technology is used to facilitate the self- and peer-assessment activities. We started by highlighting why self-assessment procedures are relevant, how technology can suitably inform this process, and what cautions should be taken over its use. Next, we shared a set of technological tools typically used by sport educators, and we explained how they can be applied in practice. Finally, we presented practical examples of how sport educators can scaffold the self- and peer-assessment of learners using technology.

Notes

1 Peer-coaches can observe their peers' game-play or excessively self-conscious learners can choose to examine their individual performance privately.
2 For example, in a basketball fast break outlet pass, the on-the-ball player needs to notice the space that the receiving teammate has in front of him and the position of potential opponents. Checking the position of players

who have fallen behind that player in the rebound will divert attention on key component in need of improvement in the quick fast break passing.

References

Casey, A., Goodyear, V. A., & Armour, K. M. (2017). *Digital technologies and learning in physical education: Pedagogical cases* (A. Casey, V. A. Goodyear, & K. M. Armour Eds. 1st ed.). London: Routledge.

Harris, L. R., & Brown, G. T. L. (2018). *Using self-assessment to improve student learning* (L. R. Harris & G. T. L. Brown Eds. 1st ed.). London: Routledge.

Moore, W., & Fry, M. (2017). Physical education students' ownership, empowerment, and satisfaction with PE and physical activity. *Research Quarterly for Exercise and Sport, 88*(4), 468–478.

Pol, J. v. d., Volman, M., & Beishuizen, J. (2010). Scaffolding in teacher–student interaction: A decade of research. *Educational Psychology Review, 22*, 271–296.

Potdevin, F., Vors, O., Huchez, A., Lamour, M., Davids, K., & Schnitzler, C. (2018). How can video feedback be used in physical education to support novice learning in gymnastics? Effects on motor learning, self-assessment and motivation. *Physical Education & Sport Pedagogy, 23*(6), 559–574.

Sparkes, A. C., & Smith, B. (2014). *Qualitative research methods in sport, exercise and health: From process to product.* Abingdon: Routledge.

Xun, G., & Land, S. M. (2004). A conceptual framework for scaffolding Ill-structured problem-solving processes using question prompts and peer interactions. *Educational Technology Research and Development, 52*(2), 5–22.

Additional resources

Casey, A., Goodyear, V. A., & Armour, K. M. (2017). *Digital technologies and learning in physical education: Pedagogical cases* (A. Casey, V. A. Goodyear, & K. M. Armour Eds. 1st ed.). London: Routledge.

Koekoek, J., & van Hilvoorde, I. (2019). *Digital technology in physical education. Global perspectives.* Abingdon: Routledge.

Index

Milton Keynes UK
Ingram Content Group UK Ltd.
UKHW050144260424
441726UK00013B/63